IS ANYBODY HAPPY?

is anybody happy

A study of the
American
search for
pleasure

NORMAN M. LOBSENZ

1962

Doubleday & Company, Inc., Garden City, New York

For
MARGERY,
who says *she's* happy

Wherefore we call pleasure the alpha and omega of a blessed life. Pleasure is our first and kindred good.

—Epicurus, *Letter to Menoeceus*

"I fly from pleasure," said the prince, "because pleasure has ceased to please."

—Samuel Johnson, *Rasselas, or The Prince of Abissinia*

Acknowledgments

Words of thanks are in order to my friend Robert Stein, who first caused me to become professionally interested in the subject of pleasure; to Gilbert Cam and the New York Public Library for the privilege of working at a sequestered desk; and to my wife, Margery, not only for the traditional spousal moral support, but also for her editorial counsel.

CONTENTS

I   *The Enormous Playground*   13

II   *The Conspiracy Against Relaxation*   21

III   *A Revised Theory of the Leisure Class*   35

IV   *No Time for Happiness*   49

V   *The Hard-Working World of Fun*   67

VI   *The Playing Fields of Industry*   83

VII   *The Most of Everything*   105

VIII   *The Pleasures of the Senses*   119

IX   *Some Masks of Pleasure*   141

X   *The Trials of Travel*   153

XI   *The World of the "Pleasure Neurotic"*   165

XII   *The Search for Pleasure*   179

Chapter I

THE ENORMOUS PLAYGROUND

The first thing that strikes observation is an uncountable number of men, incessantly endeavoring to produce the petty and paltry pleasures with which they glut their lives.

—DE TOCQUEVILLE, *Democracy in America*

WHEN I was in grade school, in the years when children were taught such arcane and fusty subjects as spelling and geography, we all looked forward to recess time. Schools were built something like prisons, then; you entered the grim fortress at 8:30 A.M. and, to all intents and purposes, said farewell to the outside world. Lacking expanses of greensward and bins of playthings, we spent recess running around a concrete courtyard where we clapped blackboard erasers in one another's faces, simultaneously releasing childish energies and giving ourselves incipient silicosis. As I remember, we had a ball.

This chalk-dusty scene came back to me recently when I visited my son's school. On the enormous outdoor playground —studded with such an elaborate array of gymnastic equipment that it could well be mistaken for the site of the Olympic games—a group of third-graders were at recess. Most of them were playing hard. But off at one side a small girl wandered aimlessly, on her face glowing no smile of pleasure, and from her mouth coming no childish shouts of glee.

"What's the matter?" I asked her.

"Oh," she said disconsolately, "now is when I have to enjoy myself."

If it is true that little children shall lead us, this one has a substantial head start. For she evidently senses at a tender age what her elders have not quite yet comprehended: the peculiar shapes that pleasure is assuming, and the cheerless functions it performs, in the culture of today. Paradoxically, enjoyment is increasingly elusive at the very moment that it appears, superficially, to be everywhere for the taking.

It is strange that this should be so. Americans have been called a lot of things; but if we had to choose a single adjective to convey to the conventional man from Mars what kind of a people we really are, that adjective might well be "fun-loving."

The simulacra of pleasure are all about us. Our public personalities wear only one expression: a grin. Our national Mecca is Disneyland. In a recent poll a group of tourists were asked: "Where would you most like to go if neither time nor money mattered?" More of them wanted to go to Disneyland than wanted to go on a trip around the world.

To be a national hero in these happiness-ridden days, a celebrity must personify pleasure. Gone are the stern idols of yesterday—the tight-lipped titan of industry, the somber statesman, the humorless orator, the solitary inventor—men of action who fired the nation's youth with dreams of accomplishments and high purpose. In their place the comedian, the movie star, the sports hero, the international playboy are enshrined—dedicated to the promulgation of the belly laugh, the batting average, and the wolf call. The ancient Greeks, who pioneered in the entertainment business, had a god for all this—Comus, the patron of mirth and revelry. Poor Comus! He hit his peak a few centuries too soon. Toga-ed, rose-crowned and torch-bearing—an amphora of laughs—he would have been a natural for network television.

What is guaranteed to win friends, influence strangers, gain business success, and make you irresistible to the opposite sex? A smile; a friendly, open, guileless smile.

What faculty is wished for most by all right-thinking people? A sense of humor. To be accused of lacking one is the unkindest cut of all; actually to lack one may be grounds for an investigation of one's Americanism. (To be realistic about it, however, the sense of humor seems to be yielding to the growing pomposity and self-righteousness of our times. A hundred years ago the people who followed the "This Way to the Egress" sign in Phineas Barnum's circus, and found themselves not in the presence of another wonder but out in the street, laughed at the trick. Today a goodly percentage of those people would promptly report the matter to the Better Business Bureau.)

At any rate, the important thing nowadays is to have fun, or to look as if you are having fun, or to think you are having fun, or at least to make believe you are having fun. The man who is not merry is suspect. A recent cartoon in *The New Yorker* catches the mood impeccably. Against a background of cocktail-party hilarity a woman accuses her glum-faced husband: *"They're* all enjoying themselves. There must be something wrong with *you."*

None of life's little rituals is too insignificant to be *enjoyable*. The mildest *divertissement* is ballooned into a wild delight; the simplest pleasure becomes an ecstasy. Advertisers, never slow to sense a trend, have leaped on the burbling bandwagon, and there is now hardly an artifact or an activity that is not intimately connected with spine-tingling happiness. Brushing your teeth—with a certain toothpaste, of course—is "fun." Cutting the grass—with a certain lawnmower—is "exciting." Do you want to know "the real joy of good living?"

Drink a certain beer. The newest jet plane is "relaxing." No product is too mundane for overtones of bliss. Soapflakes give "glamorous" suds. It is "fun" to paint your house with so-and-so's paint. Eyeglasses are "bewitching." Light bulbs are "romantic." Yeast suddenly becomes "fun to knead and braid." Building materials are "festive." Soft drinks are "sociable." Kitchen appliances are "smart." Anything you buy that is made of shining aluminum will "mirror your laughter." Even paying the bills for all these items is "a pleasure" if you have an account at a certain bank.

You may think there are some things that cannot possibly be merchandised on the pleasure principle. Graves, for instance. You would be wrong. I have in front of me an ad for a cemetery. In the illustration a smiling family of five—including two young children—are gazing fondly about the burial grounds. The copy calls attention to the "particularly attractive" sites, to the "natural beauty" of the surroundings, to the "distinctive bronze memorial plaques set level with the well-kept grass," to the "wide lawns, handsome sculpture, graceful fountains and flower-bordered paths pleasing to all."

One can hardly wait.

So great has grown our passion to turn every human activity into fun that we have painted ourselves into a vocabular corner. There simply aren't the words, any more, to express just how happifying things can be. Life is no longer permitted to be just "pleasant"; it must be "fun-bright." Days may not be merely "gay"; they must be "gayer," though gayer than what is not made clear.

In linguistic desperation we have grabbed at the suffix "rama" and tacked it on at random to helpless words to create joyful superlatives, as blindfolded children pin tails on the donkey. Stores don't have sales; they have "sale-o-ramas." Is there a special on bananas? Then it is a bananarama. You bowl at the bowlarama, drop off your dirty laundry at the cleanorama, go to the movies to see a horrorama. In case you still do not realize that you are living it up every moment of the time, you are continuously assured by all the media that you are having a funarama.

Whether we take part willingly in the self-deception or are high-pressured into it, the result is much the same. Most people are, most of the time, involved in *doing* something that will presumably give them enjoyment. By extension, the majority of us have come to equate mere busyness with pleasure. It is surely significant that in surveys made of the leisure-time activities and preferences of the American public, most persons cannot think of any activity they *dis*like.

Yet if they like to do everything, or if everything is at least tolerable, then nothing is the fun that fun used to be, originally.

Leslie Stephen, an English essayist, said of this hyperactivity:

"We do something which we have been taught always to consider as a convivial proceeding, and fancy that we are in a high state of enjoyment. Nothing is easier . . . than to deceive people about their own emotions, and to cheat them into a belief of their own happiness. This is the difficulty that lies at the bottom of all our conventional modes of enjoyment . . . We go on stupidly suffering, in the sincere conviction that sixty minutes of weariness and vexation of spirits make up an hour of happiness."

Here lies, presumably, the only rational explanation for the enthusiasts who immolate themselves at cocktail parties; for the human lemmings who clog the highways every Sunday; for the vacationists who come home bankrupt, weary, and disillusioned but who insist they have had a marvelous time; and for all those who in pleasure's sacred name go to night clubs, museum lectures, adult education courses, carpentry clinics, football games in the rain, and guided tours of glove-making factories.

Now, it is the fashion to be concerned about the ways in which we are using, or enjoying, our Leisure (capital L). They (capital T) are worried about the Problem (capital P) of what we are going to do with it. ("They" are the customary analyzers of society, the professional worriers who live on the Problems that infest Mankind as tickbirds live on the insects that infest hippopotami.) It is true that we are probably the first highly developed civilization in history to have more time for pleasure than for work. Not only is the amount of free time increasing; it is intruding and encroaching on the time for labor. It is becoming increasingly hard to tell when free time actually begins or ends; the worlds of work and leisure are gradually merging, like lovers moving slowly into an embrace.

"They" are alarmed. Dr. Boris Pregel, a former president of the New York Academy of Sciences, and a very busy man himself, took time out not long ago to predict that in a world where the application of automation and atomic energy would shortly cut the work-week to twenty hours, "the poverty-stricken will be replaced by the leisure-stricken."

Granted, all these are weighty problems. But I submit that there is another worry which deserves attention; that, in other words, all these worriers are not worrying *right*. Apart from the fact that being leisure-stricken will hardly seem like a fate worse than death to those afflicted by it, Dr. Pregel's concern stops short of the true mark. After all, when Leslie Stephen scathingly denounced the unimaginative and self-delusory pleasure bents of his countrymen, the year was 1869. Englishmen were working sixty and more hours a week. Thus, it is not so much the crisis of increasing leisure that we should be worrying about.

What we should be worrying about is whether we are getting any pleasure from our leisure—are we having any fun?

The predicament of the little girl in the school playground was not caused by the existence of recess time, but by the fact that she did not know what to do with it. It was a small vacuum in the otherwise well-ordered schedule of her day. Now the dwindling hours of work, the labor-saving devices of the home, threaten to create a vacuum for adults.

The American, like Nature, abhors a vacuum. As a result, he is increasingly engaged in an heroic effort to fill it. And filling it he is. More people are indulging in more activities, going more places, and spending more money buying more things than ever before.

The trouble is that only an infinitesimal fraction of this freneticism equals fun. Behind the masks of gaiety hides a growing incapacity for true pleasure. Worse, it is an incapacity intensified by the manic search for enjoyment that is at once its cause and its result.

The pleasure-seeker in a leisure-drenched America is like Dante nervously strolling the meadows of Paradise; he is a stranger in a Heaven of his own design.

"What are you doing here?" Beatrice asks him fiercely. "Don't you know this is the place where man must be happy?"

Chapter II

THE CONSPIRACY AGAINST RELAXATION

Be idle, be very idle. The habits of your mind are such that you will necessarily do much. But be as idle as you can.

—COLERIDGE, *in a letter to Robert Southey*

SURELY a man has never more subtly caught the tenor of his times than has Fred A. Williams, of Akron, Ohio. Mr. Williams recently obtained a patent on what he calls a "meditation aid." He describes the device as a band of metal or plastic which is bonded to a hollow strip of foam rubber. This band fits snugly against the face and the forehead, shutting off all light and thereby, as Mr. Williams averred in his patent application, "facilitating contemplative meditation." And for anyone so much a victim of the hurly-burly of the age that he cannot meditate without stimulation from the outside, Mr. Williams offers an optional bit of equipment. It permits the wearer of the band to turn a knob and thus bring into his dark ken a picture or symbol outlined in phosphorescent paint.

That such an object could be conceived, let alone regarded as of sufficient value to the community to permit its being patented, is a clear indication that moments of peace and quiet simply do not occur in the normal pattern of our lives. At the same time it bespeaks the very real yearning that exists among us to be detached, even for a brief moment, from our daily collisions and collusions with pressure and speed. It hints at our pent-up desire and unsatisfied need for a habit of relaxation which can to some extent compensate for the obsession to fill every moment with efficient and productive activity.

Contemporary heroes in best-selling novels spend the better part of several hundred pages searching for a way out of the rat race. Confessions from suburbia proclaim disgust with and rebellion against the incessant demands on time and energy. City folk seek country retreats. We barricade our assaulted senses behind tinted glass, air-conditioning, and soundproofed walls and ceiling. (But we cannot escape sound. Even when we outrun it in a jet plane, at Mach 1 it retaliates thunderously with a sonic boom.)

We make rules for ourselves: "This weekend we're staying home and taking it easy." "Next summer we're going to hole up in a little cabin; no more running around the country." "I told my wife—from now on, never make social engagements two nights in a row." But these well-intentioned codes last about as long as New Year's resolutions. We are always trying to head up a lazy river, but the current runs too swiftly the other way.

The current obligation of the American is to be eternally occupied. We are all mailmen, letting neither snow nor rain nor gloom of night deter us in the swift completion of our self-appointed rounds. Admirable as this may be in the world of work, it is not necessarily so in the world of pleasure. The concept of "free time," as the sociologists label leisure, has become by its very existence a challenge. To most of us, free time is something that has to be filled up; a blight that must be excised. One survey of the leisure hours of several hundred families discovered that most of them regularly took part in from fifteen to thirty recreational activities. A few families "relaxed" by participating in as many as seventy-four different activities!

It is significant that Americans characteristically ask what you "did" in your leisure time; they seldom think to ask what you did *not* do. It is not the same the world over. The German poet Heine once told his friends he was leaving for a brief vacation. When he returned, they asked how he had passed the days.

"I gave audience to my fantasies," said Heine, and no one thought his answer was in any way peculiar.

Today, however, contemplation has become a casualty of the battle against boredom. "We read poetry as we would a detective story," says critic Andrew Greeley. "We listen to opera, chamber music and symphonies while we do the morning dishes or prepare income-tax statements . . . Our nation has so much leisure time that it has a 'leisure problem,' and yet it lacks the essential leisure of contemplation."

The idea that *in*activity can be just as admirable and pleasurable as activity is rarely admitted. One reason for this, of course, is economic. As we shall see in more detail in a later chapter, the mathematical increase in leisure time among all strata of Americans has created a broad and rich market for the manufacturers and purveyors of pleasure products and services. This market must, like a young garden, be lovingly tended. A demand must be created and re-created for these products and services in every American breast.

The best single way to do this—in this era of conformity —is to spread the word that not only is life quite intolerable without them (perhaps not even respectable) but also that "everybody" is avidly using them, and surely *you* want to be included. A recent institutional advertisement hailing the country's "outstanding appetite for the good life" proudly proclaimed that "The average American now has the equivalent of 180 days off a year—and he was never busier!" After rapturously detailing the billions of dollars spent on boats, bowling balls, water skis, restaurant tips, and souvenir ashtrays by people in motion, the copywriter grudgingly admitted that "in some American homes, leisure is still *leisurely*" (italics his!). But, he hastened to add, this doesn't mean it can be enjoyed for free. "Sedentary leisure has its economic impact, too," he wrote, regaining his ebullient tone.

Not only must the products themselves be relentlessly promoted; the image of "active leisure" must be boosted just as intensively. Magazines, for example, regularly compile elaborate brochures for the edification of potential buyers of advertising space. A glance through them will suffice: their aim is to show that their readers are almost exclusively men and women who have nothing but money and time with which to indulge themselves. Their indulgence, however, is always active. If they are not doing something themselves, they are strenuously going somewhere to watch someone else doing something. Ideally, I suppose, 50 per cent of a magazine's readership should be going to watch what the other 50 per cent do.

It is probably safe to say that in this one-dimensional realm of advertising promotion, nobody is ever sedentary. For example, a recent pamphlet produced by *Esquire* magazine profiled its ideal man of leisure in all his choreatic glory: "a man with an ear for music . . . a taste for fine food and drink . . . an urge to participate in sports . . . an eye for photography . . . an instinct for joining . . . a flair for entertaining . . . a hand for the helm of a boat . . . and, not least, a little wanderlust to see the world."

Nothing, be it noted, was said about this modern St. Vitus *enjoying* all these things. He simply spends his substance on them.

One element in the conspiracy against relaxation, then, is this attempt by business to turn leisure into personal profit by what C. Wright Mills has called the "mass production of distraction."

Another element in the conspiracy is the national obsession with time. If the United States were to need a new symbol for its Great Seal, nothing could be more appropriate than a stop watch rampant on a field of just-closing bus and elevator doors. In a nation devoted to the idea of leisure it would seem logical that the qualities most to be celebrated would be languor, inertia, quiescence—perhaps even phlegm and sloth. In essence, all these create an aura of calm repose. But the qualities we do celebrate, as is well known, are celerity, vigor, effervescence, assiduousness, and zeal. It is not for nothing that Americans are the main exponents of time-motion studies.

"There are people," the philosopher Irwin Edman wrote, "who have never known a moment's sense of leisure until they have missed a train or a plane or had to wait in a strange town for a delayed one. In desperation they begin to look about them, to note, to fill the compulsory tedium almost as a painter or a poet might—the expression on the face of that weary or pompous or pathetic traveler, or the pattern of a group hovering over their luggage, or the outlines of some ramshackle buildings against the sky. . . ."

You might say not enough of us miss trains. Our interest is in speed, efficiency, punctuality—in the saving of time rather than the spending of it. It is interesting that the modern Greek, inheritor of a tradition of creative leisure, is still master rather than servant of time. For the Greek to hurry is to lose a bit of freedom. To be punctual is almost an insult. When a Greek invites you to dinner he does not say, "Come at such-and-such a time"; he says, "Come and see us." To specify a time, or to arrive promptly, makes it seem as if you are more interested in food than in your hosts. But Americans are misers of time, struggling to accumulate a hoard of spare moments, satisfied to know that we have heaped them up even if we do not know what to do with them.

Our ingenuity is concentrated in efforts to shave seconds. For example: Massive scientific research has produced a canister vacuum cleaner with the on-off switch on the handle of the hose rather than on the motor housing. "It turns on and off right where you are," crows the manufacturer. "Saves you the hike back to the cleaner." The "hike" being all of about five steps to the other side of the room.

Polaroid camera film now yields a finished print in ten seconds—a breakthrough of major proportions to those who felt the world was passing them by while they stood around for all of sixty seconds waiting for the old film to work.

In a new luxury apartment building on Manhattan's East Side a "taxi button" has been installed in the passenger elevators. A tenant on his way down can push the button and thus alert the doorman to hail a cab for him. The normal supply of taxis being what they are on Manhattan's East Side, especially at those times when most people would want one, the taxi button can be expected to save the tenant perhaps a tenth of a second.

In Tacoma, Washington, traffic engineers made plans for the construction of a moving sidewalk. This signals the end of the relaxed stroll. "It seems inevitable," editorialized a daily newspaper, "that one day Americans will travel on conveyor belts like clay pipes in a shooting gallery. Window-shopping will be done at a standard rate of 120 feet a minute and, if the glass-topped enclosure used in Tacoma is adopted, the finished pedestrian will emerge as pheasant under glass . . . Let automation have its due . . . but save for us the pleasure of the quiet stroll at our own pace."

After years of dedicated work, research scientists for American Airlines' jet fleet have developed an "in-flight coffee maker." It brews a pot of specially ground coffee in just three minutes—or, say, as long as it takes to fly from Baltimore to Washington. No more waiting for decent coffee until you are over Allentown, Pennsylvania.

Not to be outdone, other airlines have inaugurated in-flight motion picture showings. On long-range jet flights, first-run films are reeled off on a screen suspended from the cabin ceiling, but only in the first-class compartment. Coach passengers will just have to suffer through the empty spaces of the flying time on their own.

Even that last hallowed cliché of relaxation—reading mysteries in the hammock or French novels on the *chaise longue*—is threatened by the growth of speed reading schools. (Chocolates and bonbons, the traditional garnish for this kind of literary dish, went out long ago when the calorie counters came in.) Will the man who learns to read for business purposes at the rate of a thousand words a minute be able, if he wishes, to simmer down and savor the adventures of Perry Mason at his old lip-moving dawdle?

It is generally held, in any discussion of leisure by experts, that relaxation has been largely done in by a third conspirator: the Puritan ethic of work. This is the shibboleth from which all shibboleths on the state of pleasure in America sooner or later derive. The Puritan heritage is packaged for the trade in the form of aphorisms ("Idleness is the Devil's workshop"), preachments ("Work, for the night cometh when no man can work"), and the Sunday blue laws. Together they comprise a legacy which, the argument goes, forms one of the few remaining barriers to what would otherwise be rampant sybaritism.

One might readily be seduced into believing all this.

History is plain enough. We were settled, at least in part, by a hardy and extremely influential breed of Calvinists who provided the dour basis of our laws and customs. It is a matter of record that in Virginia in 1619 any person found idle was subjected to forced labor; that in Massachusetts games of cards, dice, horseshoes, ninepins, and shuffleboard were banned; that in Connecticut no one might smoke—the colonial fathers were concerned about wasted time rather than carcinogens—except at dinnertime; that throughout Puritan New England the law empowered constables to "search after all manner of gameing, singing and dancing"—especially "Mixt or Promiscuous Dancing of Men and Women."

There is a considerable lure to being identified with this righteous background. Who would not wish to associate himself with such an upright, rigorous tradition? Who would not choose to picture himself having a moral fiber like a steel spring—resilient yet unyielding? Ah, how fine to be tolerant of those puny beings down below who fritter away their time in play, but knowing all the same that up here on Mount Responsibility we have work to do.

The idea of this all-pervading Puritan tradition must be appealing, for it has been so widely accepted and identified with, that those in the business of selling pleasure have effectively put it to work. Motivational researchers, those self-appointed emotional Peeping Toms of advertising, have successfully harnessed the Puritan ethic of work and made it a sales gimmick. Take, for example, this Alitalia airline ad for a jet flight to Europe; it puts the anti-pleasure argument baldly:

"You leave straight from the office at 3 P.M. At 10 A.M. you're there. You haven't lost a single working day and you haven't lost a single hour's sleep."

And, presumably, you haven't had a single hour's fun or wasted time.

In this frenetic race the steamship companies labor at a disadvantage. But they struggle successfully against their limitations.

"Get to Europe in just three business days!" trumpets the United States Lines. "The world's fastest ship gets you there refreshed and ready to do your best work . . . It crosses in five days, two of which almost always come on weekends."

And if three days of non-work are still too much for flesh and blood to stand, "professional secretaries, dictating machines, and conference room facilities are readily available" on shipboard.

The ads are tastefully illustrated with photographs of leading American executives. They smile genially at the camera, but with a certain telltale nervousness about the mouth, as if they cannot wait to be up and away to the meetings and the correspondence. The moral of these advertisements and the spiritual climate in which they flourish is not lost on the ambitious executive who must travel for his firm: He who can afford the time to take a slow boat is not going to go *anyplace* fast. In short:

> Where once the bouillon and the deck chair ruled,
> Where once the captain's gala held its sway,
> Now busy men—briefcases leather-tooled—
> Work their passage in three business days.

(If the Atlantic Ocean is becoming a beehive of activity, there is yet hope for the Pacific. The advertisements for steamship lines that voyage to the Orient and the South Seas still feature dinner-jacketed gentlemen, ladies in *décolletage*, stewards bearing chilled *apéritifs*, crimson sunsets over reef-circled lagoons, and a general air of pleasing decadence. God help us all when men sit dictating while their ship pulls into Tahiti!)

Another facet of American life usually cited to prove the staying power of the Puritan heritage is the increasing use of leisure for personal advancement and improvement. Certainly there is plenty of evidence that pleasure is being subverted in the name of accomplishment (although I doubt the Puritans have much to do with it). One must, according to current folklore, improve each shining hour. At a recent convention of homemakers from all over the country, the ladies on the "leisure-time activities" panel (a grim bit of nomenclatural evidence in itself!) identified free time not with peace, quiet, and relaxation, but rather with the opportunity to "direct one's energies toward constructive projects." Probably the bluntest illustration of this approach is exemplified in a recent book titled *Leisure: 101 Ways of Making Money in Your Spare Time*. The increase in leisure time has been accompanied, too, by a sprouting of home workshops, hobby clubs, and adult education classes. Fifty million people are now registered for courses in everything from conversational Sanskrit to spot welding. Faced with an unprecedented opportunity to sit back and put our collective feet up, by the millions we have chosen to hunch over a desk and do homework.

One of the secrets of a "real vacation," according to Dr. George S. Stevenson, a psychiatrist and a former president of the World Federation for Mental Health, is to "learn new skills . . . increase your knowledge and experience. The waste of a vacation is a pitiful and even tragic thing, especially when you begin thinking of the many possibilities for turning this short time into a positive benefit." And so the most remote vacation paradise now comes equipped with golf courses, Olympic-size pools, ski runs, bridge tourneys, dancing classes —and instructors for all of these. The valley of Shangri-La, under this approach, would need an "activities leader."

Even sleep is no longer safe from the conspirators against

relaxation. A manufacturer of foam rubber mattresses urges that when we knit up our ravell'd sleaves of care, we do so "efficiently." Thus the night will not be squandered in just plain old sleep, but will be put to profitable use getting those tired muscles ready for the morrow's work.

Can we continue seriously to ascribe these attitudes—that work is inherently admirable and godly, that leisure must be put to constructive uses, that relaxation if permitted at all needs somehow to be justified—entirely to the traditions of Puritanism? The Puritans believed that the punishment of Adam—to earn his bread by the sweat of his brow—was inherited by all Adam's descendants. John Calvin carried the doctrine one step further, a most convenient step for the rising merchants of the early days of the Industrial Revolution. "Calvin's doctrine of predestination," says economist George Soule, "confirmed the Puritans in their belief that successful businessmen were instruments of the divine will in enforcing labor upon reluctant workers, and indeed in administering the whole money-making and goods-making activity of Western man under capitalistic enterprise."

True, the Puritan way of life was tailor-made to meet successfully the extreme conditions that threatened the survival of the early colonists. Ceaseless work—and, more important, a belief that work was godly—was necessary to accomplish the tremendous tasks: to clear the immensities of wilderness, to throw up shelters and defend them against hostile Indians, and to force the strange land to yield a living. There was neither room nor time for the idler or the indolent. Work was the central factor in the human vocation. Relaxation was acceptable only as a way to restore physical energy for new labors.

It seems scarcely credible, however, that twentieth-century Americans, a notoriously volatile people, are arranging their lives largely in obedience (witting or not) to a social ethic grounded in a Garden of Eden fable, structured by the environmental pressures of the seventeenth century, and refined and reinforced by the emergent industrial capitalism of the nineteenth century.

It seems highly doubtful that the executive who works his way to Europe, the stenographer who devotes her evenings to a course in World Problems, or the man who spends his weekends building bookcases, does so to keep sin at bay.

What seems a lot more credible is that the conspiracy against relaxation is at least as much a consequence of the current moral compulsion to get ahead in the world as it is a heritage of the traditional moral compulsion to work.

Today anybody with an ounce of gumption is hell-bent on being "upward mobile," which is the polite sociological phrase for keeping up with the Joneses and for stepping on their heads as one climbs past them.

"The middle classes," educator George Crothers has said—and who is not now middle class?—"are all spending leisure time trying to improve themselves in society. The idea of improving oneself has become almost as big a force in America's attitude toward leisure as the desire to 'die with one's boots on,' right on the job."

To relax rather than to move ahead is the deadly sin of the new Puritan.

Now, how do we advance ourselves these days? Not so much, sadly, by putting in long, hard, faithful hours on the job. Nor by tugging an obsequious forelock. Nor by being brave, reverent, and thrifty. We influence the people who count not so much by what we do as by the image we present. A large part of the art of public relations and industrial design is "image-making." It is, seemingly, not half so important to the progress of a modern corporation to *do* a good, decent job as it is to have a monogram for its letterhead that will convey the *impression* that the corporation is doing a good, decent job.

As with the corporation, so with the individual—on a smaller scale, of course. The big thing nowadays is not so much to *be* friendly, or honest, or competent, or industrious, or whatever other quality might prove useful, as it is to create a façade that *implies* you are these things. There is the story of the junior executive who became a senior executive by the simple expedient of arriving unshaven at the office fifteen minutes before anyone else, disheveling his clothes and hair, littering his desk with a mass of papers and a battery of empty coffee containers, and affecting a look of utter exhaustion. His image—that of stubble-whiskered, nightlong devotion to duty—was hard to ignore when the board of directors considered promotions.

The venerable work-pleasure dichotomy has been updated. The attainment of worldly success is now a moral good. Bootless pleasure—relaxation in the face of the opportunity to win this success—is now a moral evil. Clearly, idleness is not the workshop of our current Devil. Constant busyness is the satanic domain. There, out of the centrifugal whirl of activities that makes our leisure dizzy, the essence of pleasure is separated out and falls to the bottom of the Pit.

Chapter III

A REVISED THEORY
OF THE LEISURE CLASS

There is no duty we so much underrate as the duty of being happy.

—ROBERT LOUIS STEVENSON, *An Apology for Idlers*

I T IS a spring day in a year that may be any one of those sarsaparilla-and-bandstand years between the turn of the century and the assassination at Sarajevo. A chauffeur guides a touring sedan along the stately entrance road that winds to the large white house on the top of the hill. He gets out, walks smartly to the door, and rings. A maid, primly dressed in uniform and starched headpiece, opens the door. She nods, disappears, and in a few moments the master of the house emerges. He is knickered, capped, and otherwise accoutered in the sporting style of the era. A manservant follows him, carrying a golf bag filled with clubs. As the gentleman gets into his car, the chauffeur takes the golf clubs, puts them in the trunk, gets behind the wheel, and drives away.

It is clear to the veriest dunce that the local banker, the richest man in town, the social leader, and the power behind the politicians, is off for a round of golf at his country club.

Time passes.

It is now a spring day in a year that may very well be this year. A man steps out of a sparkling white split-level house set on a green lawn bordered by flower paths. He wears well-tailored sports slacks and an Italian silk sports shirt. He waves to his children, who are splashing merrily in an inflatable pool near the patio. He shoulders his golf bag, carries it to his station wagon, and drives off for the golf course.

Question: Is this the richest man in town, or one of modest means? Is he a social leader or a social nonentity? Is he a political power or a machine voter? Is he a banker, a salesman, a plumber, a poet?

Answer: You cannot tell.

In a country as homogenized as a bottle of Grade A milk, almost anyone with sufficient desire and energy, underwritten by an average amount of good fortune, can own a pleasant home, wear good clothes, drive a late-model car, spoil his children, and play at pleasures that were once the sole province of the upper classes. If the average man does not have a staff of domestic servants, he need not fear this will set him apart socially. The richest man in town probably does not have servants either, primarily because he cannot find any to hire.

Sixty years ago Thorstein Veblen, in his book *The Theory of the Leisure Class*, drew an unforgettable—and at the time immensely significant—portrait of a small group of wealthy and largely parasitical men and women whose hallmarks were the conspicuous consumption of goods and the conspicuous waste of time. In an era when only a tiny fraction of the population had either the wherewithal to accumulate "useless" objects, or a working (or non-working) schedule that permitted them to devote lavish amounts of time to "nonproductive" activities, Veblen was at pains to manifest his contempt for the leisure class, and for what he felt to be its empty scale of values.

Today, of course, discretionary time—those extra hours free

from work—is no longer the monopoly of the few. The cornucopia of the machine spews forth a superabundance of goods. As productivity per man-hour rises, the consumer may take his share of the increase in things, or in time, or in both. It has been estimated that if the average American were satisfied to live the kind of life his great-grandfather lived, he could have that life by working only five hours a week. The rest of the time he could sit at the cabin door and whittle. But over the past century Americans have taken two-thirds of their increased productivity in goods and services, and one-third in free time. And because the reduction in working hours has not been accompanied by any reduction in pay, discretionary money—those dollars which do not need to be spent for necessities—has also become more widely distributed.

The leisure class, as a result, now makes up most of the population. Pleasure-seeking, once derided as an empty pursuit, takes on major significance. Thus it becomes useful to cast up a revised theory of the leisure class.

The cornerstone of such a theory is this overwhelming fact that *the leisure class has become the leisure mass.*

When the first expedition of the Virginia Company landed its settlers at Jamestown in 1607, a group of young British aristocrats were numbered among the colonists. Some were fops, some adventurers, some idealists. All were shocked at the raw country that faced them: the miasmal swamps of the tidewater, the hostility of the Indians, the utter lack of food and shelter. But what shocked them most, perhaps, was the realization that they were going to have to work—to clear the land, build cabins, stand guard, and, on a primitive level, farm. In colonial America, it became immediately clear, there would be no leisure class. The "average work-week" would consist of every waking minute.

In time, the seemingly insuperable physical problems were surmounted. Eventually wealth and the opportunity to enjoy it came into being, and leisure became the province of a small group in whose hands this wealth was concentrated. The mass of men worked as much as eighty-four hours a week—twelve hours a day, every day—in a continuous and meaningless round of hastily eaten food, exhaustion-drugged sleep, and unsatisfying labor. As recently as in Veblen's time, the lives of the "idle rich" were still glaringly juxtaposed against an average work-week of sixty hours.

But the economy was just beginning to surge. Technological advances contributed to a vastly increased productivity. The growth of unions plus the emergence of a national social conscience combined to validate the idea that the men who labored to produce goods should also be able to benefit from them by an ever-higher living standard.

The forty-hour week arrived on the scene in the late 1930s —just in time to be kited upward again by the production demands of the World War II years. Since 1950, the average work-week has fluctuated close to the forty-hour mark. In some areas it is displaying a slight tendency to shrink still further. A survey of six million industrial workers showed that one out of six—17 per cent—work less than forty hours a week. Approximately half of all office employees are on a thirty-five-hour schedule. Many union contracts call for seven-hour days and there is much talk of—and some experimentation with— the four-day, thirty-hour week.

But the reduction in the work-week is only part of the cause for the increase in leisure time. The number of paid holidays and the length of paid vacations have increased substantially. Two-thirds of all union contracts, for example, now provide for three weeks' vacation for men with maximum seniority. A month off with pay is no longer uncommon for white-collar workers and executives. The peak of the trend to date has been reached by one Midwestern local of the International Brotherhood of Electrical Workers, which negotiated a contract calling for a one-year vacation with pay for employees with ten years' service.

When work-week reductions, more holidays, and longer vacations are added together, the total of free time mounts rapidly. A manufacturer of outboard motors—an industry that has skyrocketed with the change from leisure class to leisure mass—headlined a recent ad this way:

Two Months Vacation With Play!
Count your "days off" from May through October. Most people have 65, including weekends, holidays and vacation . . . two months of playtime! . . .

Leisure is proliferating outside the bounds of work schedules as well. Young people, for example, today seldom enter the job market as full-time employees until they reach their late teens, when they have been graduated from high school; or in their early twenties, after college and military service. But at the turn of the century more than one out of every five children between the ages of ten and fifteen were full-fledged workers. A similar trend occurs at the upper edge of the age scale. The combination of earlier retirement, made possible by Social Security and the burgeoning of pension plans, plus a longer life expectancy, is creating many extra years of free time for older persons. In 1900, for instance, a young man of twenty could expect to live another forty-two years; if he were lucky, he would be working during thirty-nine of them. Thus he had three years of retirement in prospect. Today's twenty-year-old has a life expectancy of forty-nine more years, of which only forty-three will be working years. His future holds six years of retirement. More to the point, he can look forward to being sufficiently vigorous and solvent to enjoy those years. The impact of these statistics becomes stronger if you look at them this way: In the past fifty years the average total of retirement time has doubled. If, as seems probable, the trends continue, the next generation can expect nine years in retirement.

Now, when a majority of Americans faced nothing better than a lifetime of hard work and inconspicuous consumption, it was the general understanding that leisure, and the enjoyment thereof, was a bad thing. When at the turn of the century Charles Evans Hughes, that austere minister's son and solemn statesman, was speaking in favor of a public recreation program of severely limited extent, he was forced to give his words a moral sugar-coating by talking about "the gospel of play."

True, some people envied the leisure classes; but others resented them, and both groups projected their emotions by avidly reading the society reports in the newspapers. One could vicariously enjoy Mrs. Van Rensselaer's champagne dinner for her hundred gorgeously attired guests and at the same time roundly condemn her for not using her money to support orphans. But whether the leisured few were envied, castigated, or merely tolerated, there was considered to be an undefinable aura of wickedness about them and their activities. Most people had neither the time nor the money to have fun; therefore the Puritan ethic retained its pre-eminence: work and worship were the chief pillars of social respectability.

Enter now, however, the elements of mass leisure. Pleasure becomes available to the majority. And, almost imperceptibly, the moralities are polarized.

Where it was once morally indefensible to have free time and to enjoy it, it is now morally indefensible *not* to seek leisure, and to use it for pleasurable purposes. According to the Revised Theory of the Leisure Mass, it is wicked *not* to enjoy yourself.

It has not taken too much urging for the great American public to accept this state of affairs.

For example, a thousand men were recently shown pictures of six social types. There were a jet pilot, dashingly dressed in high-altitude suit and helmet; a doctor examining X-ray negatives; a business executive with attaché case; a laborer wielding a welding torch; a socialite in top hat and tails; and a casually dressed sportsman holding a fishing rod. The members of the panel were asked which of the men pictured they would prefer to be.

To the surprise of the Center for Research in Marketing, which conducted the poll, the overwhelming first choice was the sportsman. The executive and doctor tied for second, followed by the socialite, the pilot, and the laborer in that order. The sportsman, most of the respondents said in explaining their choices, represented the carefree life of leisure, the image of vacation. The life of the socialite was considered "too fussy, confining, demanding"; that of the jet pilot, "too dangerous"; and that of the laborer, "too much work."

Commenting on the survey, the Center's president, William Capitman, said: "Time to relax, freedom from constraint, the interest and excitement of sport are the goals men seek today. The status and material success open to professional and business men are not nearly so highly valued as the . . . easy life. . . ." (But because the Center for Research in Marketing is, after all, a handmaiden for advertisers, who would certainly not sell many products if America's male population took to the woods, another spokesman hastily attempted to recoup any possibly lost ground. "One interpretation of these findings," he said, "is that, in looking for a release from the responsibilities of modern life, men are returning to primal responsibilities, the pursuit of fish and game, for example. Men who no longer bring home the bacon but a pay check are looking for more direct methods of asserting masculinity." Such as, perhaps, wearing a masculine perfume?

Few would deny that most Americans today feel there is something amiss with anyone who is not seeking and finding pleasure unalloyed. Advertisers, who presumably know what sells goods, are, as we have seen, selling all kinds of goods on the basis of the "fun" they provide. It would not be too surprising to find, some day soon, the highways dotted with billboard posters from which the bony finger of Uncle Sam points out at you to emphasize the query: *Have You Had Your Fun Today?* With "fun" incorporated at all costs into virtually every activity, the once base metal of pleasure has been transmuted into virtuous gold.

We now accept without protest the requirement to yield to our pleasure-seeking impulses, instead of to stifle them under the blanket of a puritanical conscience. Psychologist Martha Wolfenstein describes this sociological phenomenon as the emergence of "fun morality."

"Fun," she writes, "from having been suspect if not taboo, has tended to become obligatory. Instead of feeling guilty for having too much fun, one is inclined to feel ashamed if one does not have enough. . . .

"Where formerly there was felt to be the danger that in seeking fun one might be carried away into the depths of wickedness, today there is a recognizable fear that one may not be able to let go sufficiently . . . Not having fun . . . involves a loss of self-esteem. I ask myself: What is wrong with me that I am not having fun?"

The cult of fun morality may be increasingly accepted in theory. But putting it into practice is another matter. It presents almost as many problems as work morality.

For one thing, the leisure masses face not only the assign-

ment of *having* fun—they must also discover for themselves
what *is* fun. For in the absence of a true leisure class whose
activities can serve as a model—and have in the past so served
—there are none of the standard guideposts to pleasure-taking
that existed in previous societies. A result is that millions of
families, deprived of such normal cultural short cuts as a list
of handy hints for happy hours, are frantically searching for
something that, for once, isn't there: a formula for pleasure.
They are in desperation pushing all sorts of "pleasure buttons"
simultaneously, hoping to come up with a satisfactory combination.

Most of the time they are disappointed. Every study that
has been made of the use of leisure time has revealed confusion, discontent, and hyperactivity. One survey examined
the recreational activities of several hundred young families in
a Chicago suburb. All the families were busy almost all of
their free time with a wide variety of interests. Yet the typical
comment, voiced by a young housewife, was: "When I think
of the things we *aren't* doing, I get depressed." Moreover,
none of the usual differentiating factors in surveys—age, income level, geographical location—are operative. The results
are the same in all categories. Researchers studying the
leisure of New York City teenagers found only 15 per cent
who could say their use of their free time satisfied them. In
Texas, where fun is characteristically sought after on the grand
scale, more than 60 per cent of a group of top business
executives told an interviewer they were unhappy in their
non-working hours. In still another survey, a group of families
were asked to list the ten pleasurable activities they indulged
in most, and, separately, the ten pleasurable activities they
would most enjoy.

*Not one thing the families actually did appeared on the
list of things they wanted to do!*

A second burden placed upon people by fun morality is

the creation of guilt. "Reversing a proposition within the kind of moral book-balancing characteristic of our culture produces many complications," observes Margaret Mead. To rid a society of a long-ingrained ethic—to substitute fun morality for work morality—is no simple affair. The psychological habit of considering leisure as an evil to be tolerated only if it is earned by work; the habit of viewing pleasure not as a wholesome right but as a potentially dangerous reward for duty—these habits are deeply ingrained and not easily retrained.

As Dr. Mead points out, even the play of children and the retirement of the aged are tied to work. The child earns his pleasure by using play to grow and to learn; the older person is entitled to pleasure because he has already put in his lifetime of effort. The cycle of the week also fits into the earned pleasure structure. Saturday night's socializing is the compensation for the past week's endeavors. Sunday's sloth carries the moral excuse that it is a therapeutic necessity, enabling one to recharge his batteries for the labors of the week ahead.

One psychiatrist, Dr. Alan Fromme, has found it necessary to urge that people deliberately schedule simple pleasures to be enjoyed during the middle of the working week. "There is no reason to enjoy yourself only on Saturday night," he said.

Still, most of us *do* feel vaguely uncomfortable if we live it up on Wednesday evening. We are victims of the head-on clash between the traditional reward-and-punishment pattern for pleasure and the modern principle of seeking enjoyment at any time for its own sake.

This guilt is responsible for much of the current confusion over the uses of pleasure. For many people, as a result, leisure has become a time of tension rather than of relaxation. Psychiatrists are particularly aware that the spread of free time and the development of fun morality are creating emotional problems for many people. According to a pamphlet published by the Group for the Advancement of Psychotherapy, pleasure time "is the time when many people fall victim to accidents of all sorts, and when hostilities between married couples are seen to break out into the open. 'Sunday neurosis' is a common clinical entity. For children, summer vacation can be a time of great boredom and unhappiness."

But there is a third danger inherent in fun morality. And it can be infinitely more devastating than the other two. Not only is it more widespread, but this very universality tends to blind us to its existence. The danger is this: In trying so hard to fulfill this new duty to be happy, most Americans are taking the fun out of their play.

Pleasure is no longer man's servant but his tyrant.

It is perhaps not without significance that our national colloquialisms for leave-taking have gone from the Puritan "God be with ye" to the contemporary imperative: "Have fun." Notice that one does not express a *hope* that the other person will enjoy himself, nor a wish for his pleasure. One *orders* him to be merry.

For an otherwise undisciplined nation, we've been surprisingly ready and eager to carry out the mandate. If enjoyment happens to be a by-product, well and good; but the important thing is to be doing something that will pass for fun, whether or not it be counterfeit.

So we have the millions of people who go to the movies regardless of whether they want to see what's playing.

We have the millions who jump mindlessly into their cars each Sunday, heading nowhere in particular until it is time to turn around and go back.

We have the millions who turn on television each night as if they were under permanent posthypnotic suggestion.

We have the millions who give parties—and who go to parties—almost by rote, knowing they will see the same people and talk about the same things as they do at all the other parties.

We have the millions who take refuge in hobbies, and the millions who find protective coloration in clubs of all kinds.

We have, in short, what Johan Huizinga, the philosopher of pleasure, calls "false play"—play without true enjoyment. In his book on *Homo Ludens*—Playing Man—Huizinga constructs a theory of play and of its important place in contemporary culture. He sets up three criteria for true play. First, it is a voluntary activity: "Play to order is no longer play; it could be at best but a forcible imitation. . . ." Second, play involves "a stepping out of 'real' life into a temporary sphere of activity." Play is "disinterested," and "stands outside the immediate satisfaction of wants and appetites . . . It is connected with no material interest, and no profit can be gained by it." Third, true play exists only in compartmentalized times and spaces. It takes place within "temporary worlds within the ordinary world, dedicated to the performance of an act apart . . . Play begins, and then at a certain moment it is over."

Yet the overwhelming bulk of our play, or pleasure, in America today meets none of these standards. It is voluntary in name only. Fun morality places upon us the burden to enjoy; most of the rituals of pleasure we observe are imposed by external forces, from social pressures to status desires to business requirements.

Rather than being outside of "real" life, most of our pleasures are far removed from the world of make-believe; many exist solely to satisfy "wants and appetites"; many others are deliberately contrived for the sake of gain.

And, finally, pleasure has been forcibly injected into the warp and woof of our daily lives. It is so much a part of everything we do, from brushing our teeth to working at a job, that it seldom has an opportunity to exist in a place or a time of its own.

"More and more," says Huizinga, "the sad conclusion forces

itself upon us that the play-element in culture has been on
the wane . . . It becomes increasingly difficult to tell where
play ends and non-play begins."

But what about those activities which have the appearance
of pleasure?

"Modern social life," answers Huizinga, "is being dominated to an ever-increasing extent by a quality that has something in common with play and yields the illusion of a
strongly developed play-factor. This quality I have ventured to
call by the name of Puerilism, as being the most appropriate
appellation for that blend of adolescence and barbarity which
has been rampant all over the world for the last two or three
decades. . . .

"It would seem as if the mentality and conduct of the
adolescent now reigned supreme over large areas of civilized
life which has formerly been the province of responsible
adults. The habits I have in mind are . . . gregariousness . . .
the insatiable thirst for trivial recreation, and crude sensa-
tionalism. . . ."

In its own way, the dilemma implicit in the Revised Theory
of the Leisure Mass merely reflects one aspect of the basic
problem of our time: our chronic inability to use wisely the
fruits of our advancing technology.

We can give ourselves more free time than any people in
history ever had. But we then proceed to fill it with more
puerile and profligate activity than the most decadent wastrel.
Who can deny that the search for pleasure is turning into a
scavenger hunt?

Chapter IV

NO TIME FOR HAPPINESS

I know a great many men who call themselves men of pleasure but who, in truth, have none.

—Lord Chesterfield, *Letters*

IT MAY come as a shock to the professional recreationists
who can tell you exactly how many umpty-million fishing
licenses were taken out last year, and who from that
illusory figure go on to extrapolate the golden horizons of
leisure, but leisure is a commodity in extremely short supply.

According to statistics, we are living in a period of less
work and more pleasure. Theoretically, this conclusion cannot
be faulted. But, in actuality, most Americans have little time
for happiness. We work harder than ever before.

In an era fond of labeling every inequality a "gap," we may
call this difference between the theory and the practice of
time-for-happiness a "pleasure gap."

The paradox that in a period of statistically increasing leisure most of us do not have time to enjoy ourselves is one of
the most ingenious since Fredric discovered that, though years
twenty-one he'd been alive, he was a little boy of five. It en-
ables those who worry about such things to worry today about
the "leisure-stricken," who wallow without rudder or compass
in an ocean of free time; and to worry tomorrow about the

"leisure-underprivileged," who don't know where their next spare moment is coming from.

The explanation of the inconsistency is that the mathematical picture of leisure, though constructed from unimpeachable figures, is like a soufflé: underneath its seemingly solid surface are large amounts of hot air and wishful thinking. Poke it with the fork of fact and it collapses.

Statistics of free time must be read with caution, and with an understanding of the multitude of exceptions that invalidate, rather than prove, the rule. Most calculations of the leisure that Americans have at their disposal are reminiscent of those brain-teasers that start by taking the year in which Vesuvius last erupted and, after multiplying by the number of bales of cotton produced in Alabama in 1938 and dividing by the total cubic yardage of the Great Pyramid, arrive, with a flourish, at your correct age. Which, of course, you knew all along.

So it is with the data on leisure. The accountants of the good life have cast up the balance sheet to the last second, and you can take your choice of the optimistic reckonings. One estimate gives the average person 2229 free hours—93 days —of leisure a year. Another tops this with 3700 free hours— 230 days off—a year, not counting time spent sleeping. The most detailed and conservative analysis of the year's total of 8760 hours looks like this:

8 hours each day for sleep	2920 hours a year
40 hours' work each week for 49 weeks —excluding two weeks of vacation and a third week to compensate for holidays	1960 hours
2 hours each working day for travel	490 hours

3 hours every day for meals   1095 hours
1 hour each day for personal
    care   365 hours, yielding
a total of 6830 working or work-oriented hours, and a total of
1930 hours—80 days—absolutely free for pleasure.

A more enthusiastic enumerator adds fifty-two weekends,
fourteen days of vacation, six holidays, and six free hours at
the end of each working day—and comes up with a total of
180 lazy days each year. Of course if to this you append the
year's 245 working days, you come out with a 425-day year,
and the swift precession of your personal equinoxes will soon
have you planting roses in the snow.

So, like the age puzzler, the crux of the situation is that,
after all the bewildering arithmetic is over, the average person,
confronted with the alleged fact that he has X days a year
in which to do anything or nothing, boggles visibly and says
in plaintive tone:

"Who, me? Why, I don't have a minute to myself!"

Which, like his age, he knew all along.

Why he does not have a minute to himself is something
that our hero often finds inexplicable. The myth of leisure
is so firmly fixed in the national folklore that the answers,
which are as obvious as the daily facts of life, are overlooked
or ignored.

One answer is that an awful lot of people have only hearsay
knowledge of the much-touted "shorter work-week." For example, although the forty-hour week is generally regarded today as standard, the working time of millions of employees
fluctuates within a much wider range. According to a recent
study by the U. S. Bureau of Labor Statistics, there are sixty-
five million gainfully employed persons in the country. Of
these, only twenty-six million work the national average of
forty hours a week. Another sixteen million, mostly part-time

employees, work anywhere from one to thirty-nine hours a week. And a solid twenty-three million work substantially *more* than forty hours a week. Over seven million people work more than sixty hours a week.

When you come right down to it, there is no such animal as an "average" work-week. That artificial standard includes seasonal industries—mining, construction, logging, and many others—where work and free time exist in a feast-and-famine relationship. It includes thirteen million part-time workers whose appearance in the statistical tables creates a sharp deceptive drop in the "average." In addition, the "average work-week" for many basic industries is computed upon the "contract week"—the official number of hours to be worked according to the union contract—but the actual work-week may bear little resemblance to it. In Wisconsin, for instance, some paper mills have had official thirty-six-hour weeks for several years. Yet employees *normally* and regularly work forty-two hours—six of them, of course, at overtime rates. A printing crafts union has negotiated a thirty-five-hour week in some major cities, but actual hours worked average forty.

Clearly *the* work-week can be spoken of only in terms of widely varying individual experiences. Policemen, firemen, nurses, and others in similar types of employment often work a minimum forty-eight-hour week. Farmers, despite the growing mechanization of agriculture, still labor fifty to sixty hours a week. Managers and proprietors of retail businesses put in an average of fifty-three hours each week. The self-employed professional works, for the most part, a sixty-hour week. Able to set his own schedule and thus theoretically choose between work and leisure on a day-by-day basis, he permits this unique privilege to become a vicious lure that tempts him into working evenings, weekends, and holidays. And for top management executives a seventy-hour work-week is commonplace.

The man carrying the full briefcase home every evening and weekend is no less pitifully real for being a stereotype.

For some of these millions of people the long hours of work are imposed from without. But the majority put in their overtime voluntarily—either out of ambition, guilt, the desire for more money, or the sheer love of what they are doing. For instance, although the laborer, the office employee, and the skilled worker may quit promptly when the whistle blows or the clock hands reach five, millions of them do so chiefly in order to get to their *other* job on time.

About three million men and women—one out of every twenty workers in the nation—"moonlight": that is, hold a second job, either full-time or part-time. Incredibly, about 100,000 indefatigable people somehow manage to juggle three jobs within the period of twenty-four hours, thus not only moonlighting but sunlighting and twilighting as well.

Moonlighters are usually thought of as industrial employees who, having achieved a shorter workday or work-week through a union contract, take advantage of their increased leisure to earn extra spending money from a second job. But Labor Department figures reveal that fewer than one of every four moonlighters is an industrial worker. Most moonlighters are farmers, technicians, and professional men. About 40 per cent of the nation's 4,700,000 farmers have outside jobs. Some are older men or marginal operators who can make ends meet only by earning a salary. Others are young men using their second job to earn money to pay off their land or their expensive farm machinery. Some are deliberately in transition— from the farm to the city, or vice versa. One in five of the half a million men teachers in elementary and high schools moonlight to implement their low pay. Another half a million office workers, salesmen, and professional men operate their own small businesses at night. Even high-income executives moonlight. Plagued by income taxes and the constant struggle to maintain their living standards against a barrage of bills, they use their evenings to lecture, to write, or to consult for a fee.

The existence of moonlighting on this grand scale, and by this broad cross section of people, presents a challenge to those who maunder about the age of pleasure that is supposed to be spontaneously rising out of our alleged free time. It knocks cock-a-hoop the recreationists' theory that all men, given the opportunity, will gladly exchange the market place for the playground. Labor expert Joseph S. Zeisel considerably understates the case when he writes that "it is not at all clear that, for all individuals, rising income and the ability to afford more leisure will necessarily be translated into *demand* for more leisure." The fact is that most often, when the choice is available, people turn down the chance for more leisure. The International Association of Machinists recently, and somewhat petulantly, asked its one million members: "What's the use of trying to get your work-week cut from 40 to 35 hours if you're going to spend that extra leisure time moonlighting?" Certainly a union negotiator looks silly demanding shorter hours when management can point to large numbers of men eagerly working much longer than they have to.

Two nation-wide polls taken a few years ago to get a popular reaction to the possibility of a four-day work-week produced no outpouring of interest in an extra day off. Many people said they'd use the extra day to get another job; very few had any clear or rational idea about what they would do with the additional time. In Akron, Ohio, where several rubber factories operate on a six-hour day six days a week, investigators found that men called their extra leisure hours "honeydew time"— "You know, when the missus says 'Honey, do this; honey, do that.'"

Because thirty thousand men and women work this unusual schedule in Akron, the city has become a laboratory for social researchers who want to study the "threat of leisure" in microcosm. They have made no ironclad deductions. The six-hour-day people are a minority even in Akron itself. The city is an amalgam of immigrants from other sections and has little cultural homogeneity. And no thorough study has been made of what passes for pleasure in Akron. Nevertheless, some results are clear. There is an enormous amount of moonlighting, with one out of five rubber workers holding a second full-time job in contrast to the national ratio of one out of twenty. Another two out of five have some kind of part-time work.

Why doesn't the ordinary man take advantage of his new-found leisure to enjoy "the good life?" For one thing, previous experience with America's roller-coaster economy has made many men fearful that the good life may not last forever. For another, the good life often takes the form of material goods—furniture, cars, television sets, cameras, sporting equipment—which cost a lot of money.

Researchers find that the bulk of Akron's moonlighters are concentrated in two age groups. One comprises men who remember the Great Depression of the 1930s. The veterans of bread lines and apple selling are taking no chances. The threat of automation, the antipathy toward the older worker, and the growing pool of what seem to be permanent unemployables are clear warnings to them to make it while they can. The other large group among the moonlighters are young family men whose needs and appetites, for everything from milk to motorboats, grow by leaps and bounds. So do their installment debts. It does not seem paradoxical to them to spend leisure time earning money to buy things to enjoy in their leisure time.

But what about those in the upper echelons of the hierarchy of work? Surely they take time for happiness?

A favorite character of Haitian folklore is a genial jester

named Ti Malice, whose comments on life are compounded, as his name indicates, of shrewd observation and barbed humor. Among Ti Malice's stock of sayings is this one: "If work were a good thing, the rich would have grabbed it all long ago." But Ti Malice is becoming a victim of epigrammatic obsolescence. The word may not yet have reached Haiti, but those at the top of the heap *are* grabbing all the work, and putting in the longest hours. (The rest of us, as we have just seen, thinking that perhaps we may have been wrong all along, are snatching at what is left.)

August Heckscher, the director of the Twentieth Century Fund, raised the same question in the context of modern realities. "If free time is so highly prized today," he asked, "why don't the most influential citizens appropriate more of it? If free time is something to get, why don't those who get most of what there is to get, get more?"

The answer is that the tools and techniques of technology, which freed the mass of men from the need for excessive labor, have kept the noses of the few closer to the grindstone. Machines can ease the burden of production. But not until that distant future when electronic brains become infinitely more sophisticated than they now are will the increasingly complex chores of management be lessened, or the creative functions of the professional man be rendered superfluous. At the same time, these avatars of industry are not entirely self-sacrificing. They are goaded by ambition to compete for wealth and power. They chase the will-o'-the-wisp, success.

The extent to which executives shut away everything in life except their work is indicated in a survey of several hundred company presidents that was made by the American Management Association. Almost every one of a top executive's waking moments, it revealed, is utterly devoted to his job. His intense concentration on work begins at breakfast: either in the form of reading the business pages of the morning newspapers, or in breakfast meetings where he must appear clear-eyed, alert, and ready to negotiate before he has had a cup of coffee. By 8 A.M. hotel restaurants all across the country are crowded with close-shaven, impeccably dressed executives, already complete with attaché case, laying the groundwork for the affairs of the day.

The executive's lunch is, of course, a business lunch five days a week. It may be a paltry sandwich and a paraffined container of milk at his desk, or a lavish spread at a lush restaurant or in the executive dining room—in either case the man mechanically chewing and gulping is aware of the food and drink only as fuel for energy or necessary lubricant for the progress of the discussions.

At day's end the executive faces a decision: to work late at the office, eating a makeshift desk-top dinner to sustain him through the long reaches of the evening's labor; or to rush for the commuter train, hardly waiting to be seated before poring through the avalanche of onionskin memos, and at home to have a quick drink, a quick dinner, and a quick interchange with his family before going to his study to read business journals and office reports until midnight and after.

What brief leisure the executive does permit himself is similarly work-oriented. His trips are nearly always business trips. His vacations—and the majority take only two or three weeks a year—are business vacations. About half of all vacationing executives keep in constant touch with their offices by phone and mail. Many arrange their itinerary to enable them to make "surprise" social calls on customers. Some carry files and dictating machines with them on vacations so they can feel that the time away from the office is not a total loss. Normal leisure-time activities are tightly keyed to business pursuits. Golf matches, summer houses, boating trips, fishing and hunting excursions, cocktail and dinner parties at home— all are used primarily for purposes of business entertainment.

Few executives ever take an occasional day off; only office boys have expiring grandmothers.

Family life is almost unthinkingly brushed aside in favor of the job. One executive said he takes his young son to the office with him on weekends so they can "get to see something of each other." Though these men work as much as eighty and ninety hours a week, the majority said their major problem was "not enough time." Not, as you might think, time to be with their family or to relax; they were complaining about not having enough time for business.

Almost all of these men conform to what they assume is the obligatory expression of pipe dreams. They all want—they say—to "get away," to "take a long boat trip," to "spend more time with the wife and children." But let us—and them—face facts. These are men who earn an average of $68,000 a year at an average age of only fifty-one. These are men who can arrange their own schedules. In terms of time, money, and freedom of choice they can pretty much do what they please. And if they please to utter platitudes rather than to act, the conclusion is obvious.

"The fact is," concludes the survey, "executives *like* being fully committed to a job even at the expense of other pleasures." And I respectfully call your attention to the bias shown by the researchers in the use of that word "other."

If the theoretical world of leisure man thus exists largely in the statistical tables, it is nevertheless undeniable that the average American has more time free from work than his grandfather had. But Grandpa, in the scant hours of respite that were granted to him, went home and relaxed. When the early trade unions were battling to win the ten-hour day, a major tenet of their cause was a man's right to "return to his family in season with sufficient vigor to pass some hours in the cultivation of his mind." Today, we go home after seven or eight hours only to face pressures far more demanding than those of our jobs. We plow the restful hours back into work, or unreasonable facsimiles thereof.

Among the definitions given for "leisure" in the Oxford Dictionary is this: ". . . a period or spell of unoccupied time. Now *rare*." One suspects the ironic lexicographer is among that multitude of men whose evenings and weekends are fragmented into an unending series of social, educational, and civic duties and responsibilities. The pattern of life these days is such that arrival home from work is a sign not for that delicious, gradual running down of the bodily clock that ends in refreshing sleep, but rather for a frustrating summoning up of new energies to carry one through the evening's activities.

I can remember my father coming home from work, leisurely washing up, changing into comfortable old clothes, taking as long as he liked over dinner, and then wandering into the living room faced with no greater chore than deciding whether to spend the evening reading, going to the neighborhood movie, playing a game of checkers, or listening to the radio (no television in those days). Young fool that I was, I used to think how boring it must be to spend the evenings thus.

Today I know better. My generation comes home from work, takes a quick shower, and changes not into comfortable old clothes, but into a freshly starched shirt and a business suit and shoes. We dine hastily, for duty calls. One night, perhaps, a meeting of the school board or the Parent-Teacher Association. The next, an adult education class in conversational French, in case we ever have time to go to France. A third evening will be given over to "good works"—canvassing for the community fund or a national charity, or repairing toys for the children's ward of the local hospital. Church activities, social or business, are good for at least one night every other week. On Thursday evenings the Great Books discussion group meets; (this week we are to analyze the implications for modern life of William John Locke's *Essay on Human Understanding*, and *they're meeting at our house and I haven't even read the damn thing yet, and we're all out of club soda!*). Into each life one bowling night must fall—husband-and-wife teams, of course—and also an evening dedicated to entertaining (or being entertained by) people whom for the most part we have absolutely no desire to see. And so the week flies, and somewhere we must fit in fixing the refrigerator door that doesn't close and taking down the storm windows; and it would be nice to talk with the children once in a while.

Did you say something about going to a movie on the spur of the moment, or about staying home and reading a book? Don't be silly; there isn't time.

What happened in the last thirty years? Why could our fathers, who worked fifty-four hours a week, find time to relax while we run around like a chicken with its head chopped off?

One of the things that happened, oddly enough, was the increase of what we might term "official" leisure. Without the five-day, forty-hour week, there wouldn't be any suburbia. No one in his right mind would commute two hours a day to a job that began at 8 A.M., didn't end until 6 P.M., and required his presence for four hours every Saturday. But with the shortened work-week people moved out of the city—the great, big, anonymous city, where any citizen who showed up at a school board meeting or a city council session would get such a dirty look from the politicians that he would wisely not show up again. People put down roots in the suburbs. And the tender little plant grew into a kind of community Venus flytrap, enfolding each householder in a sticky envelope of organizational chores.

There is no time off for good behavior. On the contrary, the more dutifully one submits to the demands on his free time, the more demands are made. "We've found a sucker!" they say. "Don't let him go!" Nor is there any allowance made for the pressures that a man may be under in his daily work. Again, on the contrary, it is the men with the most important, the most exacting, and the most wearing full-time jobs who are "honored" with the chairmanship of fund drives, the presidencies of chambers of commerce, and the trustee-ships on village boards.

Such are the obligatory uses of what is called free time.

The busy American male is unlikely to get much construc-tive sympathy from his helpmeet. She, too, is caught up in the same familiar rat-race. Little further proof is needed after you consider the fact that a conservative national magazine published in all seriousness a major article on the problem of young wives who are too tired to make love.

What substitutes for leisure with the American female is the "leisure look"—the little casual dress, the spike-heeled play-shoes, the shorts, the carefree hair-do. She may be frazzled to a fare-thee-well internally, but on the outside she is the very model of a modern matron-general.

It is true that today's housewife has a plethora of helpful handy household aids. Prepared foods, synthetic fabrics, sur-faces that are stain-resistant, commercial services that deliver baby formula, push-button sprays that do everything but put out the garbage—all of these free huge chunks of milady's day from once time-consuming chores. Electric appliances have sharply cut the hours required for housework. But mod-ern woman may have traded her birthright for a mess of wat-tage.

The goodwife of a previous generation knew she was needed at home to keep her family functioning. She knew it because it took virtually every waking moment of her time to cook and clean and wash and sew and iron for them. She was weary, but she had a sense of fulfilling a purpose. She was "just a housewife"—that phrase which feminists denounce as a vilification of the fair sex—but at least she had an identity and a sense of satisfaction that many women lack today. She was not, perhaps, a prime mover in her community, but she was a prime mover in her home. Her husband and children appreciated her because they could *see* the efforts she made on their behalf. Nowadays the tendency among husbands and children is to make light of mother's work. How often does today's housewife hear those exasperating phrases: "Well, all you do is toss the clothes in the washer and push a button!" Or, "How come you're tired, with all those machines to do the work for you?" Or, "Don't bother to help Marcia with the dishes; she just puts them in the machine, no trouble at all."

It is little wonder, then, that today's wives and mothers find scant satisfaction in their normal role of homemaker. With more free time, their sense of purpose has given way to a sense of doubt.

"Certainly modern conveniences have freed me from heavy work," a woman friend said to me recently. "Now all I have is about a million petty tasks that aren't even honest labor. I wonder if I'm really carrying my share of my marriage."

A mother of two children, seeking information on day nurseries because she was about to take a job, found the nursery fee would be nearly as much as her salary. "If it's worth that much money to take care of my youngsters, I'll do it myself," she said. "I only wanted a job because I didn't think I was worth anything at home."

Frustrated by a so-called leisure that is not truly leisure, denied her traditional identity and purpose by labor-saving devices and techniques, modern woman finds it necessary to *do something*. She has two major outlets: community activities or a job.

Twelve million wives—one out of three in the nation—go to work. Nine million of them have children under eighteen years of age. Three million also have children under six. They earn, after taxes and expenses, very little money. They expend enormous amounts of mental and physical energy trying to dovetail their jobs with the demands of home and family. They worry a lot about whether they are doing the right thing. The working wife is often accused of seeking excitement or escape. Actually, she is seeking a sense of satisfaction and a tangible evidence of appreciation that she does not get at home.

It is interesting to note that the shorter working schedules have encouraged more women to take jobs. Two out of every three working wives have part-time jobs. Stores, offices, and plants offer special shifts for women so they can stay home until their youngsters are off to school, and return in time to prepare dinner. Who would have thought that the shorter workday would have made it possible for women to have less leisure time?

Women who do *not* work also manage to keep up a grueling pace. For them the typical day involves an endless round of community activities: PTA, church, charities, hobby groups, clubs. Clubs are particularly wearing. A study of 511 women found that they jointly belonged to 1800 organizations—an average of 3.6 clubs per woman. One housewife in Birmingham, Alabama, indicates the real scope of the enthusiast: she is a member or officer in fifty civic and welfare groups.

Are these things that one does *with* one's leisure? Or are these things one does *instead* of using leisure?

"The pause in the day's occupation is seldom the pause that refreshes," writer David Dempsey observed some years ago in the *New York Times Magazine*. "A housewife I know," he continued, "struggling to keep up with her committee work, her ticket selling and buying, her clubs, telephoning, benefits, and church activities, threw everything over for a part-time job in a book store. 'I just had to have some time to myself,' she explained."

Togetherness has already laid its clammy fingers on family time-for-happiness by promulgating the outrageous theory that nothing is really pleasurable unless it is done by the family group. "It may be asked," says August Heckscher, "why togetherness and leisure necessarily accompany each other. It would be quite possible to conceive of a state of society in which the husband, released from his work, regularly passed several hours at his club, at sports, at a cafe or bar. This happens, of course. But in American life the normal pattern is for the man to move as rapidly as the commuting facilities allow between the two spheres of home and office. The more free time he has, the more time at home. . . ."

And so we have such brainwashed attitudes as that of the vice-president of a major financial institution who likes to spend his days off washing the windows of his home with his wife and children. "It sort of brings the family close together," he says.

A new concept is about to make togetherness look like divorce. It is the idea of the "colleague family." It will, should it take hold, virtually rule spontaneous family pleasure out of bounds. It will also require a great deal of everyone's serious time and attention.

Under this concept, husband and wife would be partners in a joint career undertaking, each bringing to it their special skills. As far as the wife's functions are concerned, points out sociologist Reuben Hill, this will mean she "can no longer learn them satisfactorily from her mother's tutelage and example; they must be rationalized. Intuitive processes give way to formal rules and special technical knowledge. Moreover, the skills employed are subject to improvement as they are submitted to critical appraisal and functional selection.

"In career terms, the women's magazines provide a kind of in-service training, supplemented with the post-graduate work of the mother study clubs, the meetings with specialists at the nursery school, the cooking classes, and the growing number of handbooks for preparing unfamiliar or exotic foods . . . Planning for parenthood today includes programs of education to facilitate the understanding of children in general and one's own children in particular and thereby to help parents contribute to the maximum development of their personalities."

In short, the members of the colleague family—if they have a moment free—are going to have to go to school to learn how to be husbands, wives, and parents. If there is already so little time for happiness, what are we going to do when the colleague family obliges us to professionalize marriage?

All this choosing of work rather than pleasure points a moral: Americans *talk* about the pursuit of leisure and happiness to a far greater extent than they actually pursue them. Why?

One reason, as we have already noted, is that the morality of fun has not yet caught up with most people's consciences. Another reason, as we shall see, is that for many people the psychological guilt involved in enjoyment is too much to bear. A third reason may be that in a society geared to practicalities and success, pleasure is *im*practical.

At any rate, the notion that pleasure, like virtue, is its own reward, has not yet gripped the American imagination. We pay both ideas lip service. As we promise ourselves to be virtuous tomorrow, when presumably we will have reached a point where we can afford it, so we promise ourselves to play tomorrow, to find time for happiness tomorrow, also presumably when we shall be able to afford it. But the chances are that whenever we are offered the gift of leisure we will say in alarm, as did Dionysius the Elder:

"God forbid that it should ever befall me!"

Chapter V

THE HARD-WORKING WORLD OF FUN

When a man's busy, why, leisure strikes him as wonderful pleasure; 'Faith, and at leisure once is he? Straightway he wants to be busy!'

—R. BROWNING, *The Glove*

IT's funny, the sort of thing that catches your eye when you've been away for a long time," a foreign correspondent back home in the United States after a lengthy tour of duty overseas commented to a friend. The thing that struck him was: "Nobody falls asleep on Sunday afternoon—they all seem to be out tearing around somewhere."

The correspondent was a staff member of *Sports Illustrated* magazine, and his observation was reported in its pages. Not surprisingy, either, for the publication has a vested interest in sustained and energetic activity. A nation of hammock snoozers would provide a poor audience for advertisers of sporting equipment. But even making allowances for a reporter's finding what he is looking for, the conclusion was valid.

We *are* all out "tearing around somewhere," for ours is the era of "active leisure," when motion substitutes for emotion, and the search for pleasure becomes not a respite but a responsibility tackled as grimly as any job. The end we seek is relaxation; but the means we use often seem more likely to lead to prostration. "I'll have fun if it kills me" is the basic attitude, and quite often it does, via heart attacks, traffic accidents, drownings, and such less conventional causes of death as falls from mountain peaks or the lung embolisms that menace skin divers. But even where mortal danger is absent, there is in many of these pursuits so much hurry and scurry, so much urgency, discomfort, and sheer hard work that one wonders whether they might be adaptable to a commando training exercise.

There is a joke about the fellow who happened to walk past a tennis court and see a wizened-looking man, with white hair and pipestem arms and legs, whacking the cover off the ball. Each time that it seemed the old gaffer must surely drop from exhaustion, he would summon up some new reserve of strength and score a perfect placement. When the match was over—the white-haired man winning it with a service ace—the fascinated onlooker couldn't help going over to congratulate him.

"I hope you'll forgive me," he said, "but it's amazing the way you cover the court and hit the ball, at your age. Do you play often?"

"Every day," the white-haired man said, gasping for breath. "But if you really want to see me in action, you should watch me this afternoon in my handball match."

"*You play handball?*"

"Four-wall," said the old gaffer proudly. "You see, I believe in getting fun out of life. I get up every morning at five, run a mile through the park and take a cold shower. That gives me an appetite for a big breakfast. I get to my office at eight, work until eleven, then go to my gym for a workout—calisthenics, parallel bars, that sort of thing. At noon I have a large lunch, with a couple of cocktails first and brandy and a cigar afterward. Then back to the office until three, when I usually play squash rackets at my club. I swim ten laps of the pool there, meet a date for cocktails, dine, go to the theater or a concert, top it off with a few drinks at a night club, and get home around two in the morning."

"You do all that *every* day?" asked the onlooker incredulously.

"Well, that's just weekdays, of course. On weekends I really get moving."

"For heaven's sake, man, how old *are* you?"

"Why," said the white-haired fellow, "I'm twenty-three."

Strip away from this story its exaggeration for effect, and the picture that remains is not so far removed from the reality of the active leisure life. Not long ago, for example, nine married couples were seen spending a July afternoon playing a hotly contested volleyball game. What made the event stand out from the normally frenetic activities of American leisure was that five of the wives were pregnant.

For many years it has been customary to deplore the "spectatoritis" that allegedly infects the body of our citizenry. But those who bewail the prevalence of sedentary delights are far behind the times. Looking is steadily giving way to doing. Even those two fundamental "looking" pleasures—motion pictures and television—are being infiltrated by action. Not so long ago an evening at a drive-in movie could be thoroughly enjoyed without stirring for a moment from your car. But the newest drive-ins discourage this vegetative approach to the movies. Many have built amusement centers in the rear of the parking lot where, should the film pall, you can play shuffleboard and table tennis. A Midwestern drive-in has a pond where you can go fishing.

Television, which once encouraged utter inertia by promoting the use of remote-control devices to allow a viewer to change channels or tune his set without stirring from chair

or bed, has now come up with a development that promises
to make TV watching almost as wearing as a set of tennis.
It is a three-screen, all-channel receiver. Three different programs appear simultaneously and compete for attention. According to a newspaper advertisement for the set, "You'll be
surprised to find you can easily enjoy more than one channel
at a time. The sound is on tap in your hand control button.
When the show you are hearing drags, shift sound to another,
pick up that story and go back in time to catch the important
part of the first. Individual earphones for each member of
the family so that you can all view together but hear separately."

Now, this is more like it. No one with a three-screen, all-
channel set can be accused any longer of sitting around like a
bump on a log and taking his pleasure the easy way. The man
who has to keep track of three different plots, be alert to
anticipate climaxes, and make instantaneous and irrevocable
programming decisions—such a man is hard at play.

If Americans are suffering from any "-itis" nowadays, it is
not "spectator-itis" but "participant-itis." The unpardonable
sin is quiescence.

In recent years the amount of money spent on admissions
to spectator sports events has crept slowly to a peak of one
and a half billion dollars. The amount spent on participant
sports has zoomed to eight and a half billion dollars. The total
expenditure in 1960 for sporting equipment alone—from badminton rackets to Western saddles, from croquet mallets to
snorkels—was more than two billion dollars. At the same time
a Gallup Poll on recreation showed that half the people
queried never attended a sporting event of any kind as a spectator; on the other hand, two-thirds of them took part in one
or more active sports.

This new-found lust for exertion can be documented any
weekend in any self-respecting town. The pool, the tennis

courts, the golf course, the softball diamond—and, in winter, the sledding hill, ice-skating rink, and basketball court—will be jammed, forecasting pressure on the members of the Recreation Commission for expanded facilities. (It is significant that thousands of communities now have such a commission to organize and operate their recreational programs.)

The statistics of personal participation in sports are formidable. Between 1946 and 1960, for example, the number of people who paddled their own canoes, raced outboard motorboats, navigated cabin cruisers, or scudded along in sailboats doubled from 20,000,000 to 40,000,000. In most places it is almost impossible to find docking space in a boatyard or marina. Harbors are so crowded with permanently moored boats that there is scarcely room for a visiting craft to drop anchor. But though boating has recently become America's most popular participant sport, other active pleasures have also found increased numbers of devotees. There are 30,000,000 swimmers, 30,000,000 fishermen, 22,000,000 bowlers, 20,000,000 hunters, and 3,000,000 skiers—in each case twice as many as there were a decade ago. Nearly 8,000,000 Americans play softball; 7,000,000 play tennis and pitch horseshoes. There are 6,000,000 water skiers. There are 5,000,000 archers—most of them aiming at stuffed targets, but several hundred thousand of whom prowl the woods during special hunting seasons to bag big game with bow and arrow. According to the Athletic Institute, the only major sport to show a drop in participation is track and field. And all the increases are well beyond any proportional rise that might be expected to accompany a swelling population.

We are not only *doing* all these things: we are forever trying to do them better, faster, higher, longer, bigger, deeper. The sense of speed and urgency with which we imbue our actions is one of the first things foreign visitors to this country notice, but to us it is second nature, so deeply ingrained that

musicologists say American orchestras play classical composi-
tions at a higher pitch and 10 per cent faster than the original
tempo called for.

"The real end which Americans set before themselves is
Acceleration," G. Lowes Dickinson observed some years ago.
"To be always moving, and always moving faster; that, they
think, is the beatific life."

Skiers, for instance, painstakingly experiment with waxes in
an effort to get an extra bit of speed on slopes which already
have been hand-tailored for lightning runs by dynamiting
boulders and bulldozing trees out of the way. Swimmers wear
foot-fins. Boats are designed to carry ever more powerful motors or an extra square foot of sail. Golf balls and baseballs
are wound tighter and tighter so they will travel farther and
farther. Tennis balls get bouncier.

The urge to compete—not only with others, but against ourselves and our previous accomplishments—is standard equipment in every red-blooded one of us. "When I was real bad at
the game," a bowling enthusiast remarked, "I didn't care so
much who won. Now, when the other guy is making strikes
and I have to sit there and watch, I just go crazy. Since I got
a little skill in it, bowling isn't fun any more. It's more like
work." Similarly, no backyard badminton player worth his salt
is content merely to knock the shuttlecock back and forth
just for the fun of it. The height of the net must be measured,
the sidelines and backlines carefully chalked in, and score
kept. Every point is fought for. Even hitting a baseball in the
backyard can now be a competitive affair. A recently patented
device can be anchored to the ground, and a ball attached to
it by a cord. The force with which the ball is hit is registered
by a ratchet mechanism.

Perhaps no one works harder at sport (except the professional athlete) than the golfer, who once strolled casually
along the fairways and did not especially care how many times

he had to hit the little ball to get it in the little hole. To begin with, if he is one of the overwhelming majority of the nation's five and a half million golfers who does not belong to a private club, he must sign up at the public links by 5 A.M. if he expects to tee off by nine or ten o'clock. Many a Sunday golfer sets his alarm clock for three in the morning, drives to the course, registers, goes back home to bed, and returns to the course a few hours later to take his place in the queue at the first tee. If he misjudges his timing and is even a few moments late when his number is called, he has to start over. Public courses are so densely populated as to make a travesty of the once relaxing game. Progress from hole to hole depends on the ability of the foursome up ahead to stay out of the rough; waits at each tee can run to half an hour or more; meanwhile the players behind press on one's heels. It is normal for a round of eighteen holes, which can ordinarily be played without hurrying in four hours, to take ten hours. Not long ago Denver put motorcycle police on the fairways to speed play.

(This kind of crowding and over-use is becoming epidemic. We are running out of space for golf courses, tennis courts, and camping sites; only a few stretches of public seashore and primitive wilderness are left; conservationists report a shortage of trout, steelhead, and salmon; wildlife is getting scarcer; in Hawaii, tourist officials, overwhelmed by an influx of visitors, are running out of flowers with which to make leis.)

But to return to the golfer: in addition to battling his fellows, he is also battling himself. For the important thing is to do better than he did the last time out: to break one hundred, or to shoot par, or to lower his handicap. To this end, the Sunday golfer often spends long grueling hours at a driving range or a putting green trying to perfect his strokes. He is, in effect, in training for his pleasure.

Last night (a bit of anonymous doggerel runs) I had a
    funny pain
And to the Doc I flew.
Said he, "That comes from overwork,
There's nothing I can do.
You need a month of quiet rest,"
He added with a smile.
"You'd better drop your golf and try
The office for a while."

A psychiatrist recently remarked that nowadays he rarely
sees patients who suffer from breakdowns caused by overwork.
"But," he continued, "I see many who are near breakdowns
because they are working so hard at enjoying themselves."
Does this fast-paced activity stem from a genuine desire for
the headlong pleasures, or from a feeling that it is somehow
necessary to have strenuous fun? Why, when the weekend
comes around, do so many of us feel that we *must* do something—anything—to enjoy ourselves?

Not for nothing do statistics show that a significantly high
percentage of family arguments flare up late on Sunday afternoons. For Saturday and Sunday form a kind of rip in the
tidal flow of the week; the currents of accumulated household
chores meet the currents of unflaggingly energetic play to
create a whirlpool of weariness. To return to work Monday
morning exhausted from the rigors of two days of leisure is
not only commonplace; it is *noblesse oblige*.

Similarly, he who returns from two weeks off with pay is
frequently heard to say that he needs "a vacation to rest up
from the vacation." Moreover, this is usually true. The American vacation is designed as a non-stop marathon over a pre-
determined course. Nothing is left to chance, to idle wander-
ings, to the vagaries of a sudden mood. The trip is bounded

by the timetable, the guidebooks, the red-line superhighways on the road maps, and the accessibility of a Howard Johnson restaurant. What counts is the number of miles covered, the number of "points of interest" seen. As a contrast let us pause for a moment to consider this description, in the *National Geographic* magazine, of a European family on a vacation trip: "Father lies under a tree; mother plays with a baby sprawled on the grass; children paddle idly in the shallows. Nobody is trying to set any records. Nobody feels any compulsion to take in 25 famous attractions of the region by suppertime. Nobody intends to exhaust himself by swimming across the lake and back to prove his manhood. Nobody even cares unduly about cooking his skin medium rare."

One reason, however, that Americans work at their play is that play has gradually become the serious business of our lives. For most people, jobs are less demanding than they used to be. The seven- or eight-hour day does not really exhaust anyone; time off has lost its function as a refueling period for mental and physical energies. But by the same token, work has become less satisfying. To compensate, we seek ever more intense satisfactions from our leisure time. "Compulsive play," as Lewis Mumford observes, "fast became the acceptable alternative to compulsive work."

Compulsive play is nothing new. It was documented in the 1920s and 1930s when Robert and Helen Lynd made their famous sociological studies of Middletown. They spelled out the frantic endeavors of the people there to cram as much activity as possible into their free time, no matter how meaningless the activity might be. It was, for instance, the normal practice of many families to take a Sunday drive fifty miles out of town and fifty miles back with no specific reason or destination. Sunday drivers today are just as much impelled to get out on the highway and *go*. But they usually manage to convince themselves that they are going *somewhere*. A Middletown study made today might well conclude that the same strange compulsion is still present, but that it has acquired a veneer of purpose. Our diversions have been equipped with motivations and goals, no matter how self-delusory.

For example, the person who takes a rambling walk in the country and idly passes the time communing with nature is considered by many to be a queer fellow. But if he has previously worked hard at learning the colors and calls of birds; and if he goes with a group to a specific area; and if he carries binoculars and a bird book; and if he concentrates on identifying various species; and if he keeps score of how many birds he saw; and especially if he sees a new species for the first time—why, then he is a bird-watcher, and not queer at all.

In the same manner, many once-simple pleasures have been turned into earnest endeavors. The whittler has traded in his willow wand and pocket knife for precut plywood and power tools. "The home workshop," Eric Larrabee points out, "is now far less likely to be a source of inlaid cigarette boxes and rustic cuckoo clocks than of substantial items of family furniture . . . Once the hobbyist was presumed to be an amateur, in the best and worst senses of the word. Now you seldom know when a hobby stops being for fun and becomes professional." The dabbler in artistic endeavors has similarly sacrificed haphazard enjoyment for the sake of accomplishment. He who paints-by-number, paints trash; but the fact that he produces a recognizable, if ghastly, scene is his pragmatic reward. Pleasure must pay off. The ceramic tile kit must yield a relatively usable mosaic coffee table. There is even a 201-needle home knitting machine on the market; the lucky woman who masters it can, allegedly, produce for her amusement a machine-made "hand-knit" sweater or a pair of socks.

Social entertaining has become the hardest play-work of all. For many, parties are not to enjoy but to use; to see and be seen; to make contacts; to create goodwill; to pay off business-incurred obligations; to put across a "soft sell." There are people who do not accept an invitation until they have ascertained whom the other guests will be; if the guests are not likely to be potentially useful, the invitation is declined. One hostess made a sarcastically forthright attempt to dispense with hypocrisy and to help her guests through that awkward early stage of finding out who did what and who was important. She attached a sign to each person's back. On it was his name, his field of work, and his specific job. Nobody was shocked. Everybody there thought it was a pretty good idea, although a few suggested she might also have given a rough idea of everybody's salary.

Perhaps the saddest victims of the fun-can-be-work theory are youngsters; for they are learning to accept it as a normal state of affairs. It is no longer news that child's play has given way to children's sports; that swimming classes in an Olympic pool have replaced the beach and the pond; that the competitive pressures of Little League baseball have supplanted the pick-up game; that children of tender ages are put on miniature skates and skis or given tennis rackets not so much to introduce them to a new world of pleasure as hopefully to start them on their way to fame, as an amateur champion, and fortune, as a professional. What *is* news—for it is a comparatively recent development—is that sports themselves are in turn giving way to other areas of achievement. It comes as shock to see an advertisement that features a photo of a boy about twelve with his bicycle, baseball glove, and bat, but who is despite these riches obviously glum. He asks, in the headline: "This is vacation?"

One would have thought so, but evidently times have changed. "The child who does not attend Vacation Bible School," says the ad copy, "is fast becoming a lonely minority. Today's modern teaching techniques bring children to Vacation Bible School eagerly, as new audio-visual aids stimulate their interest, and work-study-play projects help them learn by doing." One can almost hear the childish voices piping, "Don't make me play baseball or ride my bike any more; I want to work-study-play with those new, exciting audio-visual aids."

The trend is all toward "educational" camps. At a new Eastern camp talented youngsters spend their summer vacation studying advanced mathematics, science, and elementary Russian. There are scores of camps which specialize in training children in one or another exotic art, craft, or skill, from playing the bassoon to classifying arthropods. There are more scores of "work camps," where young people gaily spend their vacation building roads and houses. (Grownups, too, are increasingly using vacations to "improve" themselves. Last year two million people attended three thousand workshops during their holidays, solemnly studying the arts.)

None of this is inherently bad; most of it, no doubt, is inherently good. What is objectionable about it is that work, achievement, and personal advancement are masqueraded under the guise of pleasure. But children by now are used to the idea that fun is real and play is earnest. What *Time* magazine calls the "Organization Child, or the Boy in the Grey Flannel Sneakers," has been with us for several years. From the moment he enters nursery school at the age of three, his life is tightly scheduled for the next fifteen years. Boys and girls go solemnly from dancing class to judo class, from swimming school to riding school, doing all the things that should be pleasures as part of a workmanlike routine.

Toys, games, and books serve the same purposeful ends. The majority of books for young people today are non-fiction. Many a youngster who can tell you all about meteorology, space travel, open-pit mining, or the life cycle of the Arctic tern has never even heard of Pinocchio or Tarzan of the Apes. Among the most popular books are "career guides"—volumes designed to turn the little ones' thoughts to how they can best earn a living when they grow up; and reference books whose chief appeal is that they "will help youngsters succeed in school."

Playthings have gone down the same dreary drain. Today's toy catalogues are guaranteed to give the heebie-jeebies to anyone old enough to remember when a doll and a big red train were Santa's stock in trade. But toys and games are no longer *play*-things. They are *work*-things. And the child in the playroom learns early in life that fun is a serious matter.

Consider, for example, the Visible Woman, an authentically detailed, fifteen-inch-tall replica of the female body. It is anatomically precise; it has a removable abdominal wall and replaceable internal organs; its transparent skin is sculptured to outline the musculature; and it also comes with a *second* set of lower abdominal parts "to simulate the internal conditions of a seven months' pregnancy." It does not come, probably through some oversight, with an obstetrical forceps, but the youngster who diverts himself with the Visible Woman is well on his way to medical school.

Scientific toys are virtually as complex as their real-life models. Young people can build electronic computers, converse via solar-powered wireless telephones, construct Geiger counters, experiment with fluorescent light, study space through a telescope or unicellular life through a microscope; the latter comes with specimens of fish, worms, and amphibia ready to be dissected, stained, and preserved on slides. There is even an archaeology kit with which a youngster can pulverize his own pigments and make a totem pole just as the Indians of the Northwest did. Conceivably the time is not far off when the Home Atomic Fission Laboratory will be available at toy counters everywhere, complete with radiation detection film badges and child-sized leather aprons.

As for games—one is almost ashamed to admit one ever enjoyed Parchesi. Board games today get down to brass tacks. One gives the players a chance to own and operate their own airlines. Another offers the youngsters a chance to prosecute and defend courtroom cases "using actual legal principles and procedures." There are many games that enable the players to refight the Civil and all other wars. Unlike the simple "airplane race" and "auto race" of a previous generation, these games require mental application. It often takes an hour or two just to come to grips with the directions. But all of them have a purpose: to prepare young people for the serious years ahead. It is perhaps significant, then, that one of the most popular new pastimes is called The Game of Life. The object of this game is clear and direct—whoever becomes a millionaire first, wins.

Most of the clarion calls to active leisure and to useful pleasure come from those who, if they do not have a commercial interest in the subject, are seriously concerned about the peril of boredom. Their answer to this peril is to increase the pace of our leisure; to shoehorn more activities into the already crowded schedule; to encourage us to turn our pleasures into goals, and to head for them with discipline.

Fortunately, some Americans fall by the wayside in this stern enterprise. It may be true, for example, that 40,000,000 people go boating; but this does not necessarily mean that they are all out whipping the nation's waterways into a furious froth with their wakes. Large numbers of them use their boats for nothing more energetic than a quiet run out to the raft, where they will bask in the sun for several hours. Similarly, the fact that 30,000,000 fishing licenses are issued does not mean that all of the licensees fish; many of them can be seen drowsing in rowboats and on riverbanks, or playing a sedentary game of poker in the lodge. And, in the same vein, a lot of folks who are statistically classified as skiers would sooner be caught dead than leave the sun-warmed chalet terrace, where they sip hot buttered rum.

Yet, on balance, there can be no real doubt that our world of pleasure today is a hard-working world. What *is* in doubt is whether this is a useful development. As the pursuit of happiness evolves from a philosophic ideal to a strenuous duty, does it still perform its function of filling up the well of physical re-creation and spiritual contentment? Or does the very intensity with which we perform our pleasurable activities deplete this well?

An answer is suggested in the Book of Genesis. It tells us that "God blessed the seventh day and sanctified it: because that in it He had rested."

Chapter VI

THE PLAYING FIELDS OF INDUSTRY

How we are made for happiness—how work grows play!

—ROBERT BROWNING

SINCE we are by and large a law-abiding people, the pro-
nouncements of high courts often tend to be accepted
as basic truths. A judicial finding can reflect—and sometimes create—the social fabric of our time. Let us consider,
then, a little-known but significant dictum handed down by
the Supreme Court of the State of Minnesota in the case of
Elma R. Sweet.

Elma Sweet, a sixty-two-year-old Minneapolis woman,
slipped on an icy sidewalk while walking from the office where
she worked to a nearby store to get a cup of coffee during her
"coffee break." She hurt her leg and was unable to work for
several weeks. Miss Sweet applied for workmen's compensation. The State Industrial Commission decided she was entitled to it. Her employer, contending she was on a personal
errand outside his premises when the accident happened, ap-
pealed to the Supreme Court. The Court unanimously upheld
Miss Sweet's claim.

"Where an employee," it said, "sustains an injury while
temporarily off the premises of her employer in exercising a

right to obtain coffee during a coffee break granted to her as
one of the conditions of employment, the injury arose out of,
and in the course of, her employment."

The decision simultaneously reveals and reinforces a cultural *démarche:* the blending of work and pleasure. Labor and
leisure, antonymous since the fateful day Jehovah sealed off
Eden, are today blending into such an amorphous one-ness
that it is often difficult to tell where work stops and play
starts. There is no longer any firm line of demarcation between
the two.

American industry is becoming one vast playing field. Labor
leaders who barely a generation ago were battling for the five-
day week, or for minimally decent working conditions, now
spend much of their time and energies negotiating such fringe
benefits as paid holidays for employees on their birthdays,
free uniforms for members of the company bowling team, and
daily rest periods. The "pause in the day's occupation" has
been multiplied tenfold. In many instances it has been written
in as an integral part of the union contract. A brewery recently yielded to demands for a "beer break"—a foamy inter-
lude during which the workers may knock off and quaff a free
seidel of suds.

Perhaps no single item better epitomizes the *gemütlich*
atmosphere that prevails in the nation's plants and offices than
the growth of the "coffee break." Forty million workers drink
eleven billion cups of coffee in daily coffee breaks. According
to the U. S. Department of Labor, one out of every four
union contracts guarantees the employee's right to the coffee
break. Plants have been struck for violation of the coffee break
clause. Ninety-four per cent of the firms surveyed in one research project granted time off for caffein; half of them allowed an afternoon as well as a morning coffee break. Add it
up: two coffee breaks a day, of say fifteen minutes' duration

each, comes to three weeks of coffee drinking a year—with cream, sugar, and full pay.

But the coffee break, piped-in music (50,000,000 workers put in their shifts to the accompaniment of "canned" music), vending machine canteens, employee lounges—these are minor examples of the invasion of the workaday world by the paraphernalia of pleasure.

Hundreds of firms, large and small, have built swimming pools, athletic fields, bowling alleys, and similar elaborate play equipment for the exclusive use of the employees and their families. Many have turned privately owned forest lands into employee parks and picnic areas. Clubs of every sort abound. Industrial leagues nurture competition in everything from softball and quoits to bridge and chess. Many companies attempt to involve the employee's family as well, with ladies' auxiliaries, wives' clubs, and father-and-son groups. Some of the larger corporations have such extensive recreational programs that they require the services of a full-time director who is often a high-echelon executive.

Even the structural design of industrial plants is keyed to pleasure. Most new factories and office buildings are laid out to keep the workers happy; lots of sunlight pouring in, spacious cafeterias, posture-form chairs, desks guaranteed not to snag silk stockings, complexion-flattering lighting, and lavatories that tend increasingly to resemble the Baths of Caracalla as envisioned in a Cecil B. DeMille spectacle. (A delightful holdout against this trend is the Olivetti typewriter company in Italy. One of its manufacturing plants was deliberately built like a penitentiary so that, executives said, the workers would have no trouble "enjoying the contrast between a place where work is king, and the hours of freedom 'outside.'")

Not so many years ago the high spot of the summer for the hired hands was the annual company picnic, at which a fellow could ogle the stenos in their playsuits, and where the boss proved what a hell of a regular fellow he was by providing free beer and soft drinks, and pitching one inning in the softball game. The playing field was the municipal park, or a picnic ground down by the river.

Today the playing fields of industry are so widespread that a national organization has been set up to help companies cope with the fun part of work. The National Industrial Recreation Association is a clearinghouse of information and advice. It can advise a board chairman on everything from the proper psychological approaches to make to employees who don't want to play games, to the best way to build a tax-deductible swimming pool. The Association had only twelve companies as members twenty years ago. Today it has more than 750 member firms, most of them giants of industry. According to the N.I.R.A.'s executive secretary, over twenty-five thousand American businesses spend more than one billion dollars a year to provide recreation for their employees.

The latter have come to accept as a matter of routine and even due the golf courses, camping sites, artificial fishing lakes, and skeet-shooting ranges that the boss has had built exclusively for them. The Eastman Kodak Company plant in Rochester, New York, includes a five-story recreation building which can accommodate seven thousand pleasure-bent employees at one time. It includes virtually every form of *divertissement* known to man, from—naturally—a photographic studio to twenty automatic bowling lanes that are open eighteen hours a day.

In the light of all this it is surprising that any work at all gets done. But, then, Archimedes is said to have discovered the principle of specific gravity while sitting in his tub, and Newton to have formulated the laws of gravitation while lying beneath an apple tree.

This merging of work and pleasure is nowhere better evidenced than in the help-wanted sections of the newspaper. The evolution of American personnel recruitment techniques is a fantastic phenomenon of its own. From the days when a straw boss would arbitrarily pick a handful of workers from a crowd of supplicants, we have come to a time when it is the employer's qualifications that are more severely scrutinized than those of the potential employee. And what does the latter scrutinize? Not wages and hours, certainly. These are sufficiently standardized to leave little room for further negotiation by the average employee. He may be to some extent concerned with his security—the structure of the employee pension fund, for instance, or the retirement-pay program, or whether the hospitalization benefits will cover his wife's pregnancy. But his chief measuring rod is coming to be the extent of the pleasurable amenities the job will provide him.

"The prospective recruit," writes Reuel Denney in the *Harvard Business Review*, "evaluates the firm with respect to the residential, social and cultural milieu that it is bringing him into. As we know from the rocket-engineer ads, this may involve the prospective employer into promising everything but a next-door polo ground for Father, guaranteed admission to the book review club for Mother, and a free Indian village for the kiddies."

Horatio Alger, whose heroes cheerfully worked long hours at low pay in order to take their first steps up the ladder of success, would be appalled at this ad from a recent Sunday paper:

TWENTY MINUTES FROM THE OFFICE murmurs the headline. There is a bucolic photo of a relaxed young man standing with his hunting dog and rifle in the middle of a lush field on a sunny day. "Leisure-time fulfillment," sighs the copy seductively.

Can this be an ad for a real estate development? A private club soliciting members? A life insurance company making a pitch for a retirement income policy?

Wrong, wrong, and wrong.

This is a major electronics company pleading for engineers. It is not in any way unusual for the times. Very few help-wanted ads *require* anything of the applicant any more; they *offer* things. For the most part they offer security, short hours, and a conveniently located office. But companies fishing in the highly competitive markets for skilled labor, scientifically trained personnel and management executives are increasingly baiting their hooks with the lures of pleasure. Little is said about the job to be done unless it can be glamorized, as when, for instance, earth-bound men who design telemetering circuits of satellites are referred to as adventurers in outer space. Most of the help-wanted ads devote the bulk of their wordage to describing the nearby beaches, golf courses, and ski slopes; the proximity of theaters, restaurants, and museums; the good hunting and fishing; or the wonderful climate. The underlying theme is the plenitude of opportunity to relax, to enjoy.

"No matter what the advertisements promise, they are no joke," says Denney. "Today we find the leisure image of certain companies dominated by their location . . . The image and promise of a new kind of outdoor life in the West and Southwest can exert a powerful atmospheric effect in recruitment. There is the fantasy of California covered by 'plastic' plants where everything is clean, contained, smoke-less, workless, and leisure-ful; [where] clean-handed workers leap straight from the plant shower into the mosaic swimming pool. On the other hand, if you call a plant a 'chemical' plant, you know that it is in smoky Bayonne, New Jersey, where the oil is on the waters and the grit is on the lawn."

Location is important even *within* a city. New York firms seeking stenographers, secretaries, file clerks, bookkeepers, and other basic-function employees know they are at a serious disadvantage if their office is anywhere but in Manhattan. And, if in Manhattan, still at a disadvantage unless within easy striking distance of the big department stores, good restaurants, and commuter terminals. The help-wanted ads in the New York papers often tell more about the physical surroundings of the job than the duties to be performed or the experience required: "midtown area," "Grand Central area," "air-conditioned," "work with congenial people," "lovely office," "most luscious office in town," "work in all-glass showroom," "assist fabulous producer," "lovely law office," "exciting atmosphere," "secretary to movie producer, thrilling atmosphere where you'll meet the greatest."

It can all be summed up in that schizophrenic phrase that is the modern personnel executive's magic formula: "It's a pleasure to work at . . ."

In some ways the specialized communications of the personnel people is taking on the characteristics of what the Japanese call *asobase-kotoba*—"play-language." The verb *asobu* refers to the world of play—everything from making a trip to being unemployed to taking part in the ritualistic tea-ceremony formalities. This language, according to Johan Huizinga, is used by the Japanese to create "the fashionable fiction that everything is only play." One talks play-language when conversing with those of noble station, or higher rank, or those who for some reason are to be flattered.

"The convention is," says Huizinga, "that the higher classes are merely playing at all they do. The polite form for 'you arrive in Tokyo' is, literally, 'you play arrival in Tokyo'; and for 'I hear that your father is dead,' 'I hear that your father has played dying.' In other words, the revered person is

imagined as living in an elevated sphere where only pleasure
moves to action."

The concept can well be transferred to our current attitude
toward gainful employment: "I hear that you play working."

Much the same infusion of pleasure into work is also taking
place on the management level. The executive, too, labors
largely in an atmosphere deceptively redolent of relaxation
and play.

His office is tastefully decorated, often with wall-to-wall
carpeting and *objets d'art*. If the executive does not qualify
for a formal coffee break, it is because his secretary has a pot
discreetly brewing at all times for his convenience. At any
rate he will soon be off to a leisurely lunch in a luxurious
restaurant, or in the executive dining room. There are similar
pleasurable compensations all along the line: the use of the
company-owned hunting lodge, yacht, or private plane; the
sales convention in Puerto Rico or Paris or, at the least,
White Sulphur Springs; the membership in the private golf
or country club for which the firm picks up the tab; the
unitemized expense account for business entertainment.

It is true that stiffer income tax regulations, and audits,
are forcing retrenchments in some of these pleasure areas of
management fringe benefits. But not without wild wails from
those executives who have gotten used to having more fun
when they work than while they play. The man who dines
on steak and lobster at his daily expense-account lunch, and
lives on stew and hamburger for dinner at home, where he
pays his own bills, is already a trite character of the times.

Some of the actual techniques of management have subtly
taken on the coloration of play. Many a sales executive, for
instance, bases much of program on contests. His field salesmen, organized into teams or "playing" as individuals, compete for prizes awarded to those who bring in the most busi-

ness in a given period. Sales campaigns are themselves "sold" to the salesmen with a flurry of slogans and banners and stickers. There are even firms that specialize in "incentive planning." They design elaborate campaigns to pep up the salesmen; they organize and judge the contests; they award the prizes, which can be anything from an electric frying pan to a two-week vacation in Europe. Salesmen's wives and children are deluged with booklets showing the prizes that Pop can win if he will only get on the ball. It is all reminiscent of the intramural games at college, where spirit counts for so much more than ability.

Company conventions and trade and professional association meetings are now routinely held either in resort or glamour cities. Business sessions are brief so that the executives may not be delayed in getting to the golf course, the sight-seeing tours, or the cocktail parties. The smoke-filled rooms are often also girl-filled, for it has been revealed that some companies, aware of the businessman's need to relax his tensions if he is to work efficiently, may provide feminine companionship for this purpose.

Even the hard basic work of thinking has been turned into play through the device of brainstorming sessions. In brain-storming, executives faced with a problem need not think about it. They need not fill their minds with grubby facts and then take the responsibility of coming to a decision. No, indeedy. They can sit around and play with ideas. The whole basis of brainstorming is that you just say whatever comes into your head, no matter how silly it may sound or im-practical it may be; but somewhere in the batch of half-baked suggestions will be something that sounds as if it might possibly work, so let's try it. If it doesn't work, we can brain-storm some more next week. Brainstorming is *fun!*

Furthermore, it is not only respectable but intellectual nowadays to conceive of business management as a giant game; a serious game of course, like poker or war, but still a game, its outcome dependent not primarily on how hard one buckles down to affairs but on the imponderables of chance, the flux of possibilities and probabilities. A game is nothing without a score; and goodness knows that the score has become an essential part of business. Competitive statistics abound. It is not enough to rack up more points than your business opponents; you must outdo your own previous marks at every turn. It is a point of honor to produce more, or to sell more, this quarter than last quarter; to do better this quarter than the same quarter last year. The lines on the charts must go constantly up. It is almost enough to make one think that what this country needs is a new measure of business success which can be proven only by a chart line that goes *down*.

To crown the play of management, the annual stockholders' meeting, once an affair of immense solemnity, is increasingly being turned into a festive occasion, replete with plant tours and box lunches. (Imagine the senior J. P. Morgan gnawing on a cold chicken leg!) Some corporations hold their meetings at resort hotels and offer stockholders the chance to make the trip at excursion rates. The special trains and chartered buses carry their gay loads of stockholders like rooters to a football game, and one and all give three rousing cheers for the chairman of the board and laughingly exclaim, "All out for the melon-cutting!"

And what is the harm in all of this—in the coffee break, the company softball team, the brainstorming session, the sales contest, the convention in Boca Raton? Well, a good deal in many areas; and not least in its effect on the state of pleasure in this country.

The intrusion of fun 'n' games into the workaday world— whatever the motives behind the infiltration—has been hailed by some as evidence that we are finally learning to milk more pleasure out of life; that we are now so ready to accept and enjoy pleasure that we can morally afford to let it invade our working hours.

In my opinion, they are wrong.

The pleasure that has infiltrated the world of work is synthetic pleasure, and the employee whose play springs out of his employment is not really playing. The merging of work and play is, rather, only additional evidence that we are still *afraid* of honest pleasure—so afraid that we are subconsciously trying to weaken and demean it.

The mixture of labor and leisure serves only to dilute each ingredient, just as stirring a little white paint into black robs each of its impact and power, and yields only a neutral gray. Similarly, blending a little synthetic pleasure into work makes each less rewarding. Psychologist Martha Wolfenstein, referring to the tendency to "fuse work and fun, manifestly to make work more agreeable but in effect probably reducing the impact of fun," tells of a boy whose arithmetic textbook was called *Range Riders: Adventures in Numbers*, and had a picture of a mounted cowboy on the cover. It was full of problems along the line of: If six cowboys on six horses can round up five hundred longhorns in two hours, how many cowboys and horses would the ranch foreman need to do the job in one and a half hours?

"The traditional image of the American schoolboy," she writes, "has been that he sits with a large textbook propped up in front of him, a book representing the hard and tedious lessons which he wants to evade. And inside the textbook he conceals a book of wild west stories . . . These two books have now been fused into one. I do not know whether this succeeds in making the arithmetic more interesting. But I have a suspicion that it makes the cowboys less exciting."

The mixture of pleasure and work has not reinforced either.

Work has not become less onerous. Pleasure has simply grown less enjoyable. The employee who is propagandized by personnel bulletins and a slick-paper house organ into taking part in a company-sponsored recreation program is in roughly the same position as the motion picture actor who must make passionate love to the leading lady while cameras roll, lights blind, and the production crew hovers ten feet away. Fun isn't fun when it's part of the job.

The fact of the matter is that pleasure has become a complaisant whore on the playing fields of industry. She is prostituted, with the best of motives, to the golden idols of Plant Efficiency, High Productivity, Employee Morale, The Rising Sales Curve, Tax Deduction, and The Big Deal. Instead of being respected and accepted as the natural companion of work, pleasure becomes the debauched servant of industrial efficiency. How otherwise could any profit-conscious company, already trapped in the tightening vise of the cost-price squeeze, justify spending so much of its corporate substance on these frothy activities and appurtenances?

The trappings of pleasure that surround the executive are, in actuality, the tools of his trade. Important business is seldom conducted—at least in its preliminary stages—in offices and over desks. It is old hat that a contact established on the golf course can lead to fruitful negotiations leisurely discussed during luncheon at the Ritz, and finally firmed into a contractual agreement on a duck-hunting weekend. A study by the Harvard Graduate School of Business Administration called the luncheon table an "invaluable provider of ideas"— far more effective as a cost-saver to some companies than, say, intensive auditing of expense accounts. And when a salesman knows that only the top man in his district will be sent to the annual convention in Bermuda, sales—or at least sales efforts—are likely to rise.

So with the employee athletic fields and the bowling alleys

and the coffee breaks. As rewards for work well done, they would at least be consistent with the neo-Puritan view of pleasure. But they are not even that.

They are techniques of management for dealing with labor.

They exist not primarily for the enjoyment of the employee, but to increase efficiency and the rate of production, to minimize labor turnover, to soothe the worker's latent antagonism toward the boss, to involve him emotionally with his job, and to influence his wife and children in favor of the company.

The plaintive cry of industry for proof that its recreational programs are indeed paying off on the balance books was capsuled in the remarks of Robert G. Dunlop, president of the Sun Oil Company, at a convention of industrial recreation directors.

"It is interesting," he said, "that while we recognize recreation programs in industry as being beneficial, there is considerable vagueness in pin-pointing just what these benefits are. Perhaps this is so because it is difficult to measure . . . the relationship between employee participation in recreation programs and such indices as absenteeism, productivity, and job stability."

An attempt to make such measurements was undertaken by the National Industrial Recreation Association last year. The study, though admittedly superficial, did show that employees of companies with recreation programs had a lower rate of absenteeism and a higher rate of job efficiency and morale. It was also interesting to see that while employees with one or two children took the least part in company recreation activities, the peak rate of participation involved men who had three or more children. One might be forgiven for assuming that the plant and the office become more pleasurable in direct proportion to the square of the noise-plus-energy output in the home.

Even the coffee break, considered by most executives to be a total and infuriating waste of time, has its little gimmick. "The results of coffee consumption," says Dr. Jean S. Felton, a professor of Occupational Health at the University of California, "are seen in clearer and more rapid thinking, forestalling of fatigue, increased motor activity, and a diminution of reaction time to stimuli." It is worthy of note, perhaps, that professors do not as yet get coffee breaks.

Some personnel experts view all recreation merely as preparation for renewed effort. There have been instances of companies refusing to honor the accrued vacation time of employees who resigned. In one case a union grievance committee, protesting the ruling, was told that management considered vacations as an investment in the "physical and mental refreshment of the employee so that he could return to work with his full energies"; naturally, if the man was not coming back to work at all, there was no reason for him to have a vacation at company expense.

The logical conclusion about the infiltration of play into work has been drawn by Joseph Pieper in his essay on leisure. "A break in one's work," he writes, "whether of an hour, a day or a week, is still part of the world of work. The pause is made for the sake of work and in order to work, and a man is not only refreshed *from* work but *for* work. Leisure is an altogether different matter. The point and the justification of leisure are not that the functionary should function faultlessly and without a breakdown, but that the functionary should continue to be a man. . . ."

So much for the delightful illusion that employers, out of the simple goodness of their hearts, want their employees to have fun.

The question arises, then, why workers are willing to invest so much of their free time in recreational programs they have long since learned are devices designed not for their pleasure, but to camouflage non-pleasurable ends.

Most analysts of the social scene have taken the stand that the meaninglessness of work has involved a "sharp, almost absolute split" between work and pleasure. They point to the frustration of the creative spirit. "Alienation," says C. Wright Mills, "means that while men must seek all values that matter to them outside of work, they must be serious during work; they may not laugh or sing or even talk, they must follow the rules . . . In short, they must be serious and steady about something that does not mean anything to them."

This seems to me to be highly questionable. As we have seen, huge chunks of the employees' day is passed in drinking coffee, chatting at the water cooler, taking rest breaks. It is just *because* the work means so little to them that they are *not* able to be "serious" about it.

Thus, one answer would seem to be that on-the-job play activities offers a person one of the few opportunities to identify with his work, or to "belong" to his organization. The employee solves two problems at a single stroke. He gives both his work and his play a focal point, an imitation of purpose, a synthetic satisfaction. The willingness to merge work and play can to a large extent be explained as an outgrowth of the need of many people to find meaning in their working life.

The job, the office, is the central factor of daily experience for most men. The terror of unemployment and retirement is not solely economic. The terror is that a man without a job soon begins to feel that he is not a man at all. In one study, eight out of ten unskilled workers said they disliked their job, but would keep at it even if they didn't need the money. Without a place to go every morning, a man is rootless. He is like a new amputee; he feels the pain of something that is not there any more.

Until recently this sense of non-belonging, of emptiness, of meaninglessness, was the private agony of the man without work. But the character of work is changing to such a degree that even the busiest employee in the most productive company can experience the same deadly touch of alienation from his job. As in the midst of life we are in death, so in the midst of work we are in worthlessness.

Man may not always have been (or be) *sapiens*; but almost from the beginning he has been *homo faber*, man the maker. So says the evidence of the bits of sharpened stone and crude sticks found with the fossil remains of the earliest man-creatures. Through history, work has represented various functions of life. To the ancient Greeks, for whom leisure was a moral virtue, work was a necessary evil to be performed whenever possible by slaves. The early Christians raised its status a level or two: work to them had no real intrinsic worth; but it was God's punishment for sin, and thus useful as a scourge for mind and body. Among the first to dignify work as a way of serving God was Martin Luther. Salvation, as well as bread, he said, was now to be earned in the sweat of one's brow. Later religious variants of the Reformation singled out work as the highest ethical value of God-fearing man.

Only in the exuberance of the Renaissance had there arisen another concept of work to offset the lugubrious Protestant prospectus: the idea that work was an act of creativity man could glory in for its own sake; that work was a fulfillment of man's spirit and purpose.

There was not a sufficient amount of time available for these two concepts of work to do definitive battle for men's minds. In 1770, give or take a year or so, Richard Arkwright invented the spinning frame for the textile industry, James Watt invented the steam engine, and the Industrial Revolution was off and running.

It brought about, says Clement Greenberg, "a separation of work from all that is not work infinitely sharper and more exclusive than ever in the past." Work was thenceforth divorced not only from the fabric of life, but from the person who performed it. Work was no longer to be done by people, but by machines tended by people. Only one hundred years after Arkwright and Watt, Thoreau was observing that "the division of labor . . . divided the worker, not merely the work."

Today, as automation intensifies the trend and starts a technological revolution of its own, the separation of man from work—the employee's alienation from his job—grows sharper and deeper. The idea that labor is the only way to Heaven has gotten lost in the new religion. And the individual's sense of personal creativity and emotional satisfaction in his work has been steadily eroded.

"Neither the secularized gospel of work as compulsion, nor the humanist view of work as craftsmanship now has great influence among modern populations," writes Mills. "If there is little Calvinist compulsion to work among propertyless factory workers and file clerks, there is also little Renaissance exuberance in the work of the insurance clerk, freight handler or department-store saleslady. If the shoe salesman or the textile executive gives little thought to the religious meaning of his labor, certainly few telephone operators or receptionists or schoolteachers experience from their work any . . . inner calm . . . For the white-collar masses, as for wage-earners generally, work seems to serve neither God nor whatever they may experience as divine in themselves. There is no taut will-to-work, and few positive gratifications from their daily round."

The man on the assembly line and the man at the work-bench are giving way to machines electronically controlled by programmed tapes of instruction. The white-collar worker reels beneath the onslaught of desk computers, dictating machines, magnetic memories, copying devices. The executive punches data into a thinking machine and waits for the type-written slip of paper that will tell him what decision to make. Even where automation has not yet intruded, the sense of identity with or control over one's work is evaporating. Men make small parts of complex products; or they form com-mittees to arrive at carefully generalized minor decisions which are transmuted by unseen magic, somewhere higher up the line, into company policy.

In short, the worker—hand or brain—often needs a plant tour or an orientation session to grasp the over-all picture of which his function is such a minor brushstroke. The man who asks himself "What the hell am I doing here, anyway?" may never be able to find out.

The craftsman of the preindustrial era enjoyed his work because he had that sense of identity and emotional rapport with it that is missing today. The craftsman controlled his tools, his skills, his ideas, his product. His work was an ex-tension of himself; and, in turn, it developed that self.

The leisure of the craftsman partook of the elements of his work. Because work held meaning for him, he found pleasure in it—both on and off the job. The artisan of an earlier generation shared with his co-workers a community of inter-ests that grew out of their own desires, rather than desires that were forced upon him. He spent a good deal of time talking shop. He read or listened to what others had to say about his field of work. Today it is almost exclusively the professional or the executive who retains this attitude. And even in their cases there is more business in the pleasure than there is pleasure in the business. The shop talk, the reading of trade and technical journals, is not so much savored for the extra dimension it lends to work as it is used for profit and personal advancement, for "tips" and "handy hints."

Too, the craftsman found his social companions among men whose work interests were the same as his. Nowadays it is primarily the executive who centers his social life around his business associates, not necessarily because he *likes* them —as often as not he may dislike them—but out of fear, fawning, or the desire to get ahead. It is interesting that the industrial worker, who for advancement or profit does not need to curry favor with his co-workers, drops them like hot potatoes when the factory whistle blows. A study by Robert Dubin pointed out that only 9 per cent of the industrial workers he interviewed made social friends among the men they worked with. Another survey of informal social life, made by the Detroit Area Study, confirms these results: people socialize with relatives and neighbors three to four times as much as they do with co-workers.

But the craftsman, by and large, is no more. Craftsmanship has largely deteriorated into 'hobbies.' Perhaps the most exacting craftsmen left in the United States today are the 23,000,000 people who spend their free time putting together the prefabricated bits and pieces of scale model kits.

"It is an interesting thought," mildly observes the public relations director of one of the leading model kit companies, "that in their search for pleasure these people don't leave the chair they are sitting on because the pleasure they seek is in their own hands and minds. What is the reason," he continues, "why so many build so many? Evidently we live in a society today where few people have the opportunity of starting a project and building it by themselves. When someone sits down to assemble the plastic parts of a kit, no one is telling him that all he should do is the hull of a ship . . . that it's someone else's task to set the masts. And when the

model is completed he can honestly say, with great pride—
'Look, I built this!' "

Few passages in literature can rival this for conveying the
dark sickness of the soul of man. But we are spared nothing.
The man who can pridefully point to his model and cry,
"Look, I built this!" is told by the manufacturer in the very
next sentence that "these kits are ingeniously designed and
require little or no skill to assemble."

The picture of 23,000,000 people cementing together shreds
of plastic in an effort to convince themselves that they are
skilled and creative is saddening—or maddening—enough.

But it pales beside the unavoidable conclusion that virtually
all American industry is on its way to becoming one huge
scale model kit. And that the workers who push the buttons
to start and stop the automated machinery, and the workers
who punch data into computers and wait for robot decisions,
are similarly looking at their handiwork and crying out in
despairing self-delusion, "Look, I built this!"

It is largely to mask this delusion of creativity and purpose
in work that the elements of play have been brought into
the arena of business. But in all the accouterments of work-
world pleasures there is no sense of true enjoyment.

The sharp separation of work and pleasure that was the
familiar rhythm for previous generations made it comparatively simple for them to assign virtue to one and wickedness
to the other. Pleasure might be evil; but it was, therefore,
exciting.

"Is it," asks Martha Wolfenstein, "because we have come
to realize that the devil does *not* exist that we are able to fuse
play and fun with business . . . ? Or have we developed a
new kind of defense against impulses . . . ceasing to keep
gratification deep, intense and isolated, but allowing it to
permeate thinly through all activities, to achieve by a mixture

a further mitigation? Thus we would have preserved unacknowledged and unrecognized the tradition of puritanism."

If this is so—and it is hard to deny—then the playing fields of industry are a fraud on pleasure, like a box of dietetic candy. Or, perhaps more to the point, like an amusement park Fun House, whose grinning façade masks an arid emptiness broken only by a cost accountant working his slide rule.

Chapter VII

THE MOST OF EVERYTHING

Wherever pleasure is to be sold, I am always a purchaser.
—OLIVER GOLDSMITH, *The Citizen of the World*

INSURANCE companies from time to time send their policy-
holders handy forms in which to list, in excruciating detail, all the personal property one owns. I don't know
anybody who has ever filled out one of these household
inventories, even though it might pay off prettily when used
to prove that the dress your wife absent-mindedly left behind in that motel in Colorado *did* cost eighty-five dollars
only a few months earlier. We all have good intentions of
filling out the forms just as soon as we get a chance. But it
is my impression that there is a good deal more involved here
than mere procrastination. Perhaps, most of us are not quite
able to face up to the incredible amount of *things* with
which we are cluttering our houses, our closets, our garages,
and our lives.

The affluence of our society has already received its share
of chastisement. But what has been generally overlooked by
the denouncers of our "most of everything" approach to life
is that the possession of material goods is coming more and

more to be an accepted—and acceptable—substitute for pleasure. To have is, *ipso facto*, to enjoy.

By logical progression, to have *more* is to multiply enjoyment. Getting and spending we lay waste not only our powers but also our happiness, sacrificing it on the cash-register altars of the gods of consumption. For in the emotional shorthand of the soaring sixties the poet's "thing of beauty is a joy forever" has been truncated to "a thing is a joy"—and, should it threaten to last forever, a waste-maker can be summoned to do his stern duty.

Even the simplest joys have become festooned with what can only be called "stuff," like a Louisiana cypress tree laden with millstones of moss. Pleasure has been accessorized—a phenomenon possible only in an era of abundance.

I can remember, for example, the fun of a day at the beach when it was a more or less unpremeditated outing, and not a full-fledged expedition organized and outfitted as if for a journey to the headwaters of the Amazon. One needed a bathing suit and towel; a pail, shovel, and ball for the children; sandwiches, fruit, and milk. There might also be one or two optional items: a book or magazine, a pair of sunglasses, a sweatshirt. A really persnickety person could push together a mound of sand, pat it into shape, drape it with the towel— and presto! he had a backrest.

But watch them arriving at the beach today. Father carries —in two trips—the enormous umbrella, the collapsible table, several anodized aluminum beach chairs, and the portable grill. Mother totes the picnic hamper (complete with plastic plates, cups, and cutlery for eight), the vacuum jug, and the portable icebox. The children are laden with other necessaries: the air mattresses, the blankets, the water toys, the beach toys, the photographic equipment, and the kit with suntan preparations, nose shields, eye masks, and bathing caps. All of this is routine equipment, fairly primitive by the standards of abundance. More sophisticated excursionists set up tents and canopies, inflate the floating chaise longues and the floating coasters, break out the portable bar, turn on the portable transistorized radios and phonographs, and carry extra bathing suits, terrycloth robes, and wraparound skirts.

Not long ago investment banker Paul Mazur, hailing an economy that can support so many private satisfactions, wrote: "Take a serf who works twelve hours a day, seven days a week. What kind of life is that? He's a mole. All he needs is some burlap to clothe him, some potatoes, a pair of brogans. Now think of a family spending its leisure on the beach. The slave hasn't time to consume anything. The family on the beach has time for everything."

Mr. Mazur lost sight of one point. There is so much for the family on the beach to unpack, set up, put together, organize, operate, take apart, take down, and put away, that there is barely time for a swim.

Should you decide that a trip to the beach isn't worth all that trouble, you may join the more than 300,000 families who have built backyard swimming pools. On the surface, it is a simple proposition. Men come, dig a hole, line it, fill it with water—and *voilà!* the ol' swimmin' hole has come of age. But you have not reckoned with the necessary accessories: a filter, an automatic top skimmer, a bottom vacuum attachment, a backwash kit (for the pool, not the people), purifying chemicals, a pool cover. There are also *un*necessary accessories such as lights for night swimming, ladders, and diving boards.

Maybe you are willing to settle for a drive in the country? Be sure to have your magnetic dashboard tray to hold the coins for the tolls; the silicone spray to keep the windshield dust-free; the automatic cigarette dispenser; the plasti-cushioned headrest, the armrest, the backrest; the mapholder, the carryall, the picnic case, the tinted sun visors, and the can of compressed air to fix a flat tire.

Or perhaps you would rather just stay home and take a nap? Then you will need the blanket supporter to keep the covers from pressing on your feet; the knee cushion, to raise your knees to a flexed position; the preshaped plastic armrest; the three-way adjustable backrest, complete with elastic strap to hold your anti-allergenic pillow; and the four-position bed elevator to raise your head to the desired angle. The collapsible bed board and the mattress extender are, of course, already in place.

The truly dismaying aspect of this whole grim picture of consumerized pleasure is not that it exists, nor even that it is unquestioningly accepted; the dismaying thing is that all these impedimenta have oozed their way across the dividing line that separates luxuries from necessities, and have become trappings without which we cannot go forth to enjoy ourselves. In time, most of these devices pall. They become more of a burden than anything else. Boatyard managers, for example, are used to seeing expensive craft, originally bought with great enthusiasm, left unused and untended by their disillusioned owners. True, this may be a prerogative of the wealthy. But there are countless homes in the land whose attics and basements are cluttered with the once yearned-for, and now abandoned detritus of the abundant life. It is sad that we buy so much in the name of pleasure. But it is sadder still that so much of what we buy we do not really want.

The era of excessive abundance has diluted not only our own pleasures, but the pleasures implicit in giving to others.

Perhaps never before in history, except for absolute rulers and absolute ascetics, has there been such a person as "the man who has everything." Yet he is with us today. The reality of his existence becomes clear especially at Christmastime, when stores seek to help those of us who face the task of finding something to give him. They suggest jeweled stamp boxes, paper clips of solid gold, the use of a rented Rolls-

THE MOST OF EVERYTHING 109

Royce for twenty-four hours. Friends rack their brains to think of something he does not have. Whether or not he may enjoy it is immaterial. It does not occur to anyone that the man who has everything may not want anything more.

But to give is now obligatory. The joy of giving has been replaced by the routine of giving. The gift horse today is a puny colt, foaled by Habit out of Lists, and delivered by Merchandising. The commercialization of Christmas, with the subsequent loss of spontaneous pleasures, has been well documented. But the fun of almost every present-giving occasion has been similarly spoiled.

The storybook youngster who beams with glee at the gift of a bright red ball has gone off to Fairyland. In his place is the hard-to-please toy-smothered child. Either he already has what you brought him, or he had it and didn't like it, or it isn't like the one they advertise on television. Children's birthday parties nowadays turn playrooms into subsidiary warehouses for toy stores. If the giver took pleasure in giving, or the recipient in receiving, there might be an excuse for this potlatch. But the giving is expected and routine. And little Jimmy carelessly shreds the gay wrappings and, shortly thereafter, the playthings themselves. What difference does it make? More will be along soon.

In a different way, the pleasure has been removed from what used to be one of the most satisfying areas of gift-giving: the wedding present. There was a certain feeling of participation in joy; there was a certain challenge to find the *cadeau juste* that would reflect your truly personal wish for the happiness of the young couple. But the modern bride and groom are not particularly interested in the *cadeau juste*; they are concerned with furnishing a home. Their object is to acquire quickly and painlessly all the things that every couple needs today to start out in life. (It is remarkable, incidentally, how many things are considered vital by the young couple setting

up housekeeping. A minister once remarked: "When I offici-
ate at a wedding ceremony nowadays I often feel like saying,
'Dearly beloved, we are gathered together in the presence of
a complete set of china, crystal, silver and linens, and a fully
equipped kitchen, to join in holy matrimony. . . .'")

And so we have seen the creation of that monstrous invention, the bridal register. The engaged couple select the
patterns they like in dishes, glassware, linens, silver. The
choice is listed at a major store in town. And the wedding
guest has nothing more to do than tell the store how many
dishes or tablecloths or place settings he wants to underwrite.
If he gets a warm, glowing feeling when he writes out the
check to cover the month's charge account, he is unusual.

Columnist Dorothy Kilgallen revealed with precision, if not
elegance, the kind of thinking that is in back of this "most
of everything" approach to pleasure. Somewhere she came
across the remark made by Bertrand Russell that "To be
without some of the things you want is an indispensable part
of happiness." Characterizing this as a "nutty quote," Miss
Kilgallen then commented, "Oh, sure, Bertrand, it's marvelous fun not to have a mink coat or a nice flat or caviar to go
with the blinis."

Why have we come to accept the fact that it is *not* "nutty"
to identify blissfulness with the possession of the skins of one
animal and the eggs of another?

It is possible to find religious roots for the sense of pleasure
that comes from owning material goods. "It is part of our
Protestant heritage," a philosphy professor recently observed,
"and it goes back to the Old Testament. Wealth is the tangible evidence of God's grace, and a display of blessings proves
blessedness."

A more likely reason, however, is that most Americans
equate pleasure with material success, and success with the

possession of worldly goods. When a magazine, for example, wants to convince potential advertisers that its readers are vital and vigorous people, it does so by listing the percentage who own things. An *Esquire* brochure, for example, hailed its subscribers' "enthusiasm for acquiring a lavish accumulation of exciting possessions." These included hand and power tools, outdoor cooking equipment, camping equipment, swimming pools, color television sets, and electric organs. No books, no works of art, no musical instruments that you play rather than plug in. The measure of success—and thus the measure of pleasure—is quantity, not quality; cost, not use.

To a considerable degree this is Veblen's "conspicuous consumption" updated. Veblen pointed out that, so long as a community was sufficiently self-contained for everybody to know all about everybody else, a man could establish his social position by conspicuously wasting time. But, he said, in a world where one's neighbors are not necessarily one's friends or even acquaintances, where there are many people to whom one's social status is unknown, then—"the signature of one's pecuniary strength should be written in characters which he who runs may read . . . Conspicuous consumption begins to hold over leisure. . . ." Today we live in a world of strangers who neither know nor care about our job, our education, or our ancestry. The only way to impress this world is with a display of possessions.

But the greatest impetus toward the objectifying of pleasure came from the spread of leisure time to the majority of Americans. Millions of people, suddenly endowed with spare hours and extra days, faced the problem of what to do with them. There were few Thoreaus among them; most were ill-prepared for the assignment. By a happy coincidence, however, the new leisure—unlike the empty days of the Depression years—was accompanied by spare money, as well. Too, the modest self-denial of World War II was over: as con-

sumer goods began to flow back into the market place, it was
not only possible but also morally acceptable to buy things
for fun.

At first the dimensions of this market for fun "jest growed,"
like Topsy. Then, as if some impatient pediatrician had given
Topsy a shot of pituitary gland extract, it shot up to be-
wilderingly awesome heights. And today recreational products
and services are being bought at a fantastic rate.

The best and latest estimate of the amount of money
spent each year in this country for various aspects of pleasure
is forty billion dollars. This sum approximately equals the
annual cost of the national defense. It is greater than the
total of all personal income tax receipts. It is a Gargantuan
8 per cent of the gross national product. It includes such
fascinating figures as one billion dollars spent on backyard
pools; a quarter of a billion dollars on women's bathing suits;
twelve billion dollars on tools and materials for "do-it-yourself" projects; twenty-three million dollars on baseball gloves;
five million dollars for children's sleds, and nearly a fifth of
a billion dollars on fishing supplies. We pour one billion
dollars into bowling and another billion into hunting; two
billion into gardening, two and a half billion into boating.
Over one-third of a billion dollars goes for photographic
equipment. The outdoor barbecue craze costs one hundred
million dollars for grills and twenty-five million dollars just
for paper plates. We spend six million dollars for tennis balls,
thirty million for golf balls, and another thirty million for
sunglasses and goggles.

There is no way of telling how many more billions spent
on technically utilitarian items are actually outlays for pleasure. Most estimates of recreational spending, for instance,
exclude the annual U.S. liquor bill of twelve billion dollars;
yet most of this amount is consumed in social drinking.
Toiletries are seldom considered a leisure-time expense; yet

the millions spent on suntan lotions, insect repellents, anti-poison-ivy medicaments and similar items are clearly the result of excursions and vacations. An enormous slice of the clothing industry is devoted to casual wear and sportswear— another direct outgrowth of the search for pleasure.

New businesses were born and old ones revitalized by the surging demand for ways and means of having fun. Many fed on one another. Architect George Nelson enthusiastically described the process this way: "Golf . . . involves joining a club of some sort. Clubs multiply social contacts. Social contacts, when expanded, can translate themselves into an interesting variety of things. New dresses for parties (new hanging rods for the new dresses, new closets for the new hanging rods). New clothes and shoes for the golfer. More cocktail and highball glasses. An ice bucket. (A better refrigerator?) New porch furniture for father's new friends. . . ."

Even insurance companies—whether or not you fill out their inventory forms—benefit from this virtuoso display of consumption, for all the goodies need to be protected against everything from earthquakes to moth damage. The millions of boaters need liability insurance. The millions of skiers would be wise to buy health insurance. As one ad so delightfully put it: "A family outing can quickly turn into a nightmare when planned insurance protection is missing."

The upshot of all this is that, without anyone actually realizing it until recently, pleasure has become a major prop of the nation's economy.

Business, handicapped by its traditional obeisance to outworn clichés of economic thinking, had long overlooked the economic implications of the growth of leisure. The great god of economics had been Production. In what John K. Galbraith calls the "conventional wisdom," production was considered the "most frequent justification of our civilization, even our existence." As Geoffrey Gorer observed in *The Americans*:

"Any device or regulation which interferes with the supply of more and better things is resisted with unreasoning horror." Leisure time is non-productive; consequently, anti-economic. It was not resisted with unreasoning horror probably because it accrued piecemeal—an hour here and there, the gradual disappearance of the Saturday half-day, the slow lengthening of annual vacations.

None of these alone alerted businessmen. But suddenly they realized that substantial numbers of people had a substantial amount of free time and a substantial amount of money to spend in filling it. No longer was a tiny minority making the bulk of luxury purchases. The new leisure market was supported by thirty-four billion American families who control most of the nation's $84 billion discretionary income. And the economic function of pleasure burst like a star shell in the business sky.

That function was—to *buy*.

David M. Potter, Yale Professor of American Studies, summed up the new duty of the leisured masses:

"Americans must be taught to consume on their days off."

Mass leisure, said Potter, has created fewer producers, more consumers, and new kinds of demand for new forms of production. In short, the search for pleasure can be the great equalizer of production and consumption. "Once abundance is secure," Potter wrote in his aptly titled *People of Plenty*, "the ideal individual develops the qualities of the good consumer. He needs now to cultivate interests that are appropriate to an enlarged leisure."

And what if he fails to develop these qualities and cultivate these interests?

"Clearly," continues the professor, as if he were glad you asked that question, "clearly he must be educated . . . to perform his role as a consumer, especially as a consumer of goods for which he feels no need. The only institution we have for instilling new needs, for training people to act as consumers, for altering men's values, and thus for hastening their adjustment to potential abundance, is advertising."

The pupils are way ahead of their would-be teachers. If the classrooms are empty when the bell rings, it is because most of the students are out shopping.

But even a forty-billion-dollar bill for pleasure is not enough to satisfy the apostles of consumerism. Marketing men are distressed at the lack of the "hard sell" in the leisure-time market. A few years ago *Tide*, a marketing trade magazine, spelled this out in letters of fire and money:

"Twenty years ago people spent roughly four per cent of their income on leisure-time activities. Now they spend about the same percentage, even though they have much more leisure . . . Right in that fact lies the mightiest of markets— open to any and every comer . . . Few companies really sell it as successfully as they would or could. . . ."

And what are the basic factors for successfully selling pleasure? First, according to the experts, keep one step ahead of the consumer's wants. Second, convince him that not only the price is right, but that the product is worth a slice of his time, that it is literally "worth while." Third, the product must present the consumer with a tangible benefit, "whether it's convenience or just plain fun."

In the last several years businesses that followed these rules prospered. A large part of the lure of foreign travel is now based on the opportunity the tourist has to buy things— especially in free ports. Entire guidebooks have been written about "how to shop" in foreign countries. At home, the highest rate of increase of net income after taxes among all categories of business has been chalked up by corporations in the amusement field. Companies specializing in pleasure have rocketed to stock market leadership. Representatives of labor, far from resenting the trend, encourage it: Without the forty-billion-dollar bill for fun, the economy would go into a tailspin; therefore, they reason, we must maintain high employment and high wages to keep purchasing power up, but at the same time we must reduce working hours so that people will have the time and the desire to consume.

The salability of fun is being milked for all it is worth. The result is the application of Gresham's law to the economy of pleasure: the debased currency of synthetic happiness, irresponsibly coined by advertisers and marketers, is driving essential joys out of circulation.

Of course this trend toward substituting things for pleasures can't be entirely blamed on the hidden persuaders. The fault lies equally with those who buy. "Impaired judgment," says Gerald Johnson, "is what leads a man to the acquisition of things he does not want. David Harum's remark that, as he surveyed his life, it was not the money he had spent for good times that he regretted, but the good times he might as well have had but didn't, is exactly to the point as far as it goes, but it doesn't go far enough. David should have regretted most of all the money he spent for good times that he didn't get."

Some of the most grimly magnificent phenomena of our times have been forecast with amazing accuracy by writers of science fiction. The wonders of radar, television, solar cells, submarines, robots, electronic computers—even the entire paraphernalia of space travel, from satellite stations to G-suits for astronauts—were envisioned, named, and described by them as long ago as the 1920s.

But no one put even an iota of credence in the dreams and nightmares of these writers until the dreams and nightmares began to come true. Today Congress appropriates dozens of millions of dollars to build a huge dish antenna that will listen to the galaxy in an effort to hear signals from extra-terrestrial beings. Probe rockets circle Venus. Astronomers talk matter-of-factly about the likelihood that a billion intelligent species exist in the cosmos. We are learning to talk with dolphins. Robot machines build, operate, and repair themselves. Science fiction, once considered the province of crackpots, has acquired a bourgeois respectability.

Now, the point of all this is that science-fiction writers of the sixties are turning their imaginations from the physical worlds of future science to the social structure of the future. Again they are extrapolating grimly magnificent phenomena. And, again, nobody believes them.

Yet why not? Is it so unlikely, considering our present *Drang nach* conformity, that we may not live in the world one writer envisioned, where all men wear identical masks and communicate via stereotyped messages on flash cards? Is it so unlikely, considering what our still primitive brainwashing techniques can accomplish, that some day brain-wave technicians may be able electronically to remold a man's memories or personality at the whim of the state?

Or would it be so surprising, considering the already delicate balance between production and consumption in our economy, to find Americans living in a society that *required* them to buy a specific amount of goods and services each week, under pain of punishment? that made *consuming* the chief patriotic obligation of each individual? It would follow, then, that most people would work only a few hours a week, and spend most of their time consuming. It would also follow that the chief privilege of rank and station would be to *not buy* things—and status would be topsy-turvily established by *in*conspicuous consumption.

This kind of social structure of the future, where compulsory consumption inverts all values, has already been described by science-fiction writers. In light of the conditions that prevail today, it is quite reasonable to expect such a society to develop. How long it could last is another question. The prognosis would not be good. In the heavy words of educator Dr. William Russell: "Too much leisure with too much money has been the dread of societies across the ages. That is when nations fall."

Chapter VIII

THE PLEASURES OF THE SENSES

I know not how to conceive the good, apart from the pleasures of taste, sexual pleasures, the pleasures of sound, and the pleasures of beautiful form.

—EPICURUS, *Book X*

A BRAVE man recently commissioned a score of craftsmen to build him a bed.

It was a double bed, extra-size. It had soundproofed side walls that could be raised or lowered at will. It had a wall running down the center that was also retractable. One side of the bed was equipped with a battery of nozzles that sprayed perfume, and with an electric massage machine. The other side was fitted with an electric razor and an electric toothbrush. A screen built into the canopy over the bed was wired for motion pictures and television. Cunningly designed trays swung from concealed storage into position to hold food and drink. And a series of buttons, when pressed gently, released various scents: of flowers, new-mown hay, smoked ham, hot coffee, and fresh fish.

The man is brave because he is a hedonist, and hedonism is out of style.

One of the most significant signs of the decline of pleasure is the surprise, the shock, the embarrassment, indeed the distaste, with which we view the man or woman who unashamedly seeks to enjoy the physical world around us. The frankness of sensual diversions strikes us as unseemly. "If you must please yourself *that* way," we say, "have the decency either to do so in private, or to make believe you are doing so under protest." And so social conscience doth make cowards—or hypocrites—of us all.

Without plumping for Epicureanism unlimited, it is safe to say that to revel in the sight or sound of beauty; to relish the taste of a pungent flavor; to inhale the fragrance of an aromatic scent; to luxuriate in the feel of a fine fabric, to make forthright love—all these are rapidly becoming numbered among the lost pleasures.

Americans have not yet taken to pillar-sitting in the desert, like Simeon Stylites; nor have they, like the lion who was tamed by the ascetic Abbott Gerasimos, been converted to vegetarianism. But asceticism of a new sort *is* a cloud on the horizon, even if it is as yet no larger than a package of frozen waffles.

Today's austerities, of course, are no longer rooted in the belief that denial and suffering here on earth are the box office price of a reserved seat around the heavenly thrones. In the time of the pillar saints and the desert monks, when men inflicted tortures on their bodies as a sort of spiritual fertilizer to promote the growth of the soul, the sensory pleasures were considered temptations of the Devil. Men mortified the flesh to defeat Sin. Today the dangers are more secular. We do not refrain from pie at dinner because we look forward to pie in the sky, but because we have already had the day's quota of calories.

It may very well be that a part of the national preoccupation with calories stems not from a concern over health or figure, but from a subconscious realization that food and food preparation being what they are in America, there is not much gustatory point to eating for pleasure, anyway. In any event, for a country with the world's highest physical standard of living, Americans are among the world's most unimaginative eaters and drinkers.

Outside of a handful of high-priced establishments in or near a few of the major cities, it is virtually impossible to get a superbly prepared and faultlessly served dinner in a restaurant. More effort is expended in making the descriptions on the menu mouth-watering than in making the food itself delectable. A report by a gastronomic expert recently confirmed that the number of outstanding chefs in American restaurants is declining, and the *haute cuisine* being replaced by the steam table and the warming pan. "We either don't have the taste for or don't want to take the time for exquisite cookery," he concluded. A British newspaperman who has spent a good many years in this country agrees, more in sadness than in anger, that he knows of no nation, with the possible exception of Turkey, "where the food in public places is so completely uninteresting." From coast to coast, one is faced with dreary sameness of the "businessman's lunch" and the table d'hôte dinner: the sliver of already half-melted butter, the wilted greens, the cardboard vegetables, the rubbery fish, the leathery meat, the gelatinous pie, the fresh fruit from cans. In the Far West one runs the additional risk of finding one's steak smothered in thick gravy and served in that ghastly form called "chicken-fried." Anyone who has traveled twenty-four hours in the South knows the Big Lie about Southern cooking.

But instead of impassioned outbursts against the monotonous mediocrity of restaurant food, we get guides to "fine dining" that spend more time describing the cleanliness of the washrooms than discussing the edibility of the food. One of the finest meals I ever had was in a tiny café in the town of Weed, California, where the washroom was out of commission and the nearest substitute was a tributary of the Klamath River trickling down from Mount Shasta.

The real rape of the taste buds begins, however, at home. Take soup, for example. Once upon a time, they tell me, soups were lovingly prepared over a low flame for several days, simmering in the good flavor and meanwhile wafting savory smells about the kitchen. Then came the can. Yet it was still possible for the serious cook to use the contents of the can as an adjunct to the basic liquor on the rear burner. But then soups appeared disguised as packages of shredded fibers and in the tins of frozen mush. Now there is "instant" soup— and there is no way to go but up.

It will be a long, hard road back, though. The signs of the times are clearly discernible. The women's magazines continue their schizophrenic practice of devoting an equal amount of space to lush recipes and to crash diets; but, significantly, the recipes are buried in the back of the book, and the diets are blazoned on the front covers. The younger generation of housewives-to-be does not promise much improvement. A survey of the habits of teenage girls discovered that the dishes they could make best, and consequently liked to make most, were chocolate layer cake and spaghetti—thus presaging a pessimistic future for gourmets and an optimistic future for the creators of the crash diets.

Exoticism in food has degenerated into practical joking. Much of the business done these days by "gourmet" shops centers on such Epicurean aberrations as chocolate-covered ants and baby bees in soy sauce. "Spooky food," as the trade calls it, comes largely from Japan, and it is interesting to note this label, written with characteristic Oriental subtlety, on the back of a tin of toasted caterpillars: "The question often asked who is eating these? We reply, with great jollity, judging from the large export orders, the answer we suppose to be is largely Americans." Said a spokesman for the Japan Trade Center, also with great but diplomatically concealed jollity, "At home, we use caterpillars only for fishing."

But these are merely fringe attacks on the old-fashioned pleasure of eating. The major onslaught has come from the food merchandisers, who have successfully promoted speed, convenience, and sanitation as of far more importance than such a vulgarity as taste.

If anyone doubts that Americans are more concerned with how quickly or how easily a dish can be prepared than with how well it pleases the palate, he need only run his eyes over the food advertising pages, with their "Quik-This" and "Minit-That." Anything that takes more than four minutes to "heat 'n' serve" is doomed to dusty desiccation on the supermarket shelf.

Nor have we come anywhere near the end. A chemical company is producing a bulk cellulose which will fill but not nourish us—the first true non-food. "The meals of the future," a dairy products executive said recently, "will be prepared within moments from freeze-dried foods on microwave cooking units. Freeze-dried foods, which combine the best qualities of freezing and dehydration, will move onto the kitchen shelves with irradiated sterilized foods, more low-calorie foods, more foods packed in tubes and pressurized containers, and 'single service' units"—the latter being the home version of the blue plate special.

"Cooking," said the executive, "may become as simple as telephoning a friend, since one major manufacturer has already developed a dial control system for an electronic range that can be directed by the housewife from any dial telephone in the country."

Does anyone really care about the loss of pleasure in eating? Not really. Most people today eat as if they were ready to spring out of their starting chocks for the sixty-yard dash. There is the movie or the theater curtain to catch; or the date who is waiting in the living room; or the after-dinner guests who may show up early. About the only time food is eaten slowly is when it is eaten in the state of semi-hypnosis that accompanies television viewing. Often the evening's *piéce de résistance* is a TV dinner—and it may take a conscious effort of the will to detect when one has stopped eating the mashed potatoes and started eating the tray.

Perhaps it is just as well, the incidence of cholesterol-triggered heart disease being what it is, that Americans eat to live rather than live to eat. But drinking—surely a people who fathered the Whiskey Rebellion and who were always seeing what the boys in the back room would have, surely they still relish the trickle of golden liquids down the throat?

This country spends close to twelve billion dollars a year on alcoholic beverages. And most of it goes for potables widely advertised to have the least possible distinctive taste. The nation's most popular drinks are blended rye mixed with ginger ale, and impotent beers whose wishy-washiness masquerades as "crispness," "lightness," and "dryness"—in other words, lack of flavor. Rich, foamy, dark beers are conspicuous by their absence and unpopularity. To one who fondly recalls drinking, in Munich, a bottle of beer whose label distinctly read "29 per cent alcohol," American lager yields a pale facsimile of pleasure.

The vogue for "lightness" is not limited to beer. The rise in popularity of gin and vodka is directly attributable to the fact that they have little or no flavor. Americans prefer a sweet, light champagne to a dry, full-bodied one. The most successful brands of Scotch lately have been those with a reputation for lightness, and an entire and disturbingly successful advertising campaign has been built around the imbecilic slogan, "Scotch Me Lightly." Good wines are seldom drunk;

more than two out of three Americans do not either drink or serve wine even once during the entire year. After-dinner liqueurs—whose sharp flavors cannot be camouflaged—are hardly ever served. Brandy is for fruitcake or the rich.

When you come right down to it, Americans take very little real pleasure in their drinking. Everything has ice in it, anyway, to kill what taste may have crept in; people who drink their whiskey neat are, outside of saloons in Western movies, a small fraternity. Some years ago the *Quarterly Journal of Studies on Alcohol* published the results of a national survey that inquired into people's motives for drinking. Of nearly two thousand respondents who drank, only 28 per cent said they drank liquor because they liked it, or because it made them feel good. The rest of them drank for "social" reasons, or because they thought it was good for their health.

As with taste, so with other senses. Euclid alone may have looked on beauty bare, but he would have difficulty distinguishing her today among the geometric nightmares of modern art and architecture. The voluptuousness of Renoir, the passion of Gauguin, the exuberance of Breughel have been replaced by Pollock's random daubs, Kandinsky's scrawls, and a generation of joyless poseurs who, when we seek to feast our eyes, starve us with "Black on Black." Heroic sculpture has yielded to collages of scrap metal. It has been a struggle, admittedly, to undo the natural beauty our land is heir to; but we are nothing if not persevering in our crusade against the sensory pleasures. Thus thousands of miles of scenic wonders are hidden from view by an endless Great Wall of Pizza Palaces and Kustard Korners, Midway Diners, Souvenir Shoppes, and Sleep-Tite Motels. If any chinks are inadvertently left they will be instantly plugged by a billboard. Has it occurred to anyone that the billboards are in the wrong places? That instead of being on the highways, where only speeding motorists glimpse them, they should be on our cities' main streets? There not only could the slow-moving pedestrian read them at leisure, but they would also serve the valuable function of partially concealing not trees and fields, but the current plague of rectangular glass boxes we have allowed to be identified as magnificent edifices.

Similarly, we applaud a modern design which largely eschews sensual beauty for frigid functionalism. We meekly stipulate that the small identical crates which sprawl their dreariness across the suburban greenery shall be called attractive homes, and we opt to live in them. We willingly eat with cutlery that resembles surgical instruments, and from dishes created by a horde of plastics designers who are evidently all taking fanciful revenge on their high school geometry teachers. We sit uncomfortably in chairs designed more to be looked at than to support a human skeleton. We uncomplainingly ride in automobiles which have substituted chrome and leatherette for burnished wood and velvet plush, and which oblige us to assume preposterous spinal curvatures to get in and out of them.

The world of sound is no less a victim of the revolt against sensual pleasure than is the world of sight. The full-bodied music of the masters can scarcely be heard above the ululations of the electric organ in full vibrato. Melody and harmony are lost altogether in the dissonances of "computer music." Technicality has replaced creativity. The hi-fi enthusiast is not interested in Mozart or Moussorgsky for the passion of their music nor the grandeur of their themes. He is interested in how they sound on a certain turntable, with a certain preamplifier. Mozart and Moussorgsky have become projects in acoustical engineering.

Or else they have become part of a collection mania. Catalogues of classical music, once discreetly thin, are now obscenely fat. Have enormous new treasure houses of music been discovered? Are the less well-known but still delightful works of famous composers being rescued from oblivion? No. What is happening is that competing record companies are producing literally dozens of different versions of the same basic works, with different orchestras and under different conductors. There are now, for example, seventeen different recordings of Beethoven's Ninth Symphony. The music lover, the Beethoven devotee, might conceivably be satisfied with one or two. But the hi-fi buff must have them all. He may not—and generally does not—have much conception of the emotional content of the music. But he will be, or will pretend to be, an expert on the technical shadings: why Toscanini emphasized the woodwinds here, or Beecham speeded the violins there.

The way-out music lover does not really bother with music at all any more. He is more concerned with the gimmicks of sound. To stimulate and satisfy this craze, recording companies have produced a Beethoven *Battle Symphony* that includes 188 cannon shots and twenty-eight musket volleys in the orchestration. The armament takes precedence over the musicians on the record's cover: "Two six-pound smooth-bore bronze cannons and 12-pound howitzer, French Charle-ville-pattern muskets and British Brown Bess muskets." A record of Handel's *Fireworks Music* has a real burst of fireworks dubbed into the score. An album of Richard Rodgers' *Victory at Sea* mood music now comes complete with the sound of guns, planes, crash-diving submarines, and torpedo explosions. One may well inquire whether these records are aimed at a listening audience or at an ordnance audience.

The really up-to-date record fancier expends a great deal of effort and money to obtain the most sensitive pick-up arms, tuners, speakers, and turntables, and then uses them to listen not to music, but to the sounds of Diesel engines, or racing cars, or rain on the roof. Or he listens to test signals recorded at the lowest and highest levels of audibility. His greatest pleasure, in the end, is to sit midway between his stereo speakers and hear nothing. For then he knows he has tested his equipment to the utmost limits. His ultima Thule is now a record that yields no sound at all. Thus the sensual enjoyment of music deteriorates into the cataleptic contemplation of stereophonic silence.

But of all the pleasures of the senses, none is so much on the downgrade as the sexual. It seems to be an official tenet of the American way of life that as much pleasure as possible should be removed from the sexual relationships between men and women.

Are you in love? Analyze your feelings, don't just enjoy them. How dare you wander hand in hand under a June moon to the top of Observatory Hill when you should be making discussion lists for your premarital counseling session?

Do you enjoy sex? How can you be sure unless you have tested your Sex Knowledge Inventory Quotient, and measured your performance techniques alongside the statistical norms?

Is your marriage going along happily? Ah, that is just what *you* think. Read the women's magazines, and Dr. Clifford Adams and Dr. David Mace and Dr. Paul Popenoe and all the other doctors will tell you what may be wrong with it.

There is not even much enjoyment left in falling in love. There seems to be insufficient energy or gumption for the fever in the blood, the passion that brooks no bounds, the "craving void" of Byron which "drives us to intemperate but keenly felt pursuits . . . whose principal attraction is the agitation inseparable from their accomplishment." The pleasures of profligacy are dying. Casanova, bounder though he may have been, was "in love" each time he claimed a boudoir triumph: or convinced himself he was, which is as good as the reality (and often *is* the reality). But the dullest clod of a seducer nowadays knows he is motivated not by love, nor even by *toujours gai,* but by psychic impotence or oral eroticism or sado-masochistic tendencies. The lovers in our allegedly highly-spiced modern literature are mousy, wistful, or, worse, egocentric. Their adventures grow either out of alcohol, vanity, or a sense of mild obligation. Affairs in real life seldom are fired by any of the grand passion that excuses them. They are dispirited misadventures, conducted without flair or dash; brief encounters of flesh. Love more often stems today from boredom than from ecstasy, and yields more guilt than pleasure. Thus we can laugh at the joke about the would-be adulterous couple who, having furtively registered in a hotel, are suddenly overwhelmed by remorse as they stand outside the bedroom door. "If I hadn't paid for the room already," says the hero, "I'd say let's forget about the whole thing."

To all intents and purposes, romantic relationships of whatever degree of intensity should be pleasurable, re-creative. The very history of language calls for it. The Sanskrit word for "play"—*kridati*—is often used in the erotic sense; *kridaratnam,* the literal translation of which is "the jewel of games," means sexual intercourse. In almost all ancient and modern tongues the word for "play" or "pleasure" has sexual connotations.

"The view that sex is fun," writes social philosopher Nelson Foote, "can hardly be called the invention of immoralists; it is everyman's discovery." But it is more than that. It is also implicit in the sexual mechanisms given to mankind.

Only human beings have the physiological and psychological capacities to experience sex as an emotion in and of itself, apart from the instinctual imperatives of reproduction and the preservation of the species. Only human beings are equipped to respond sexually to symbolic and ideational, as well as biologic, stimuli. Only the human female, almong all females, is able to respond to sexual advances at any time she desires, rather than only at periods of ovulation.

But in the face of these God-given privileges, we retreat. "Rather than finding how to use sex in a fulfilling way," writes family life authority Lester A. Kirkendall, "we have concentrated on trying to confine sexual activity to a minimum through the use of warnings and threats of dire consequences. The average adult is so ashamed of sex, and so fearful of the sexual impulse and its manifestations that he is . . . afraid to display any genuine interest in it. These actions make it impossible for us to live happily with our sexual impulse. . . ."

So we become increasingly determined to deny the spontaneities of love and sex; to substitute thought for feelings and analysis for enjoyment, whether we are dealing with the preliminary delights of dalliance or the deepest intimacies of marriage. We have managed, finally, to outflank the pleasures of love and sex, and to dehydrate them into a series of statistical tables and sociological theories. We no longer fall in love, or make love. We interrelate.

According to the quarters in which the definitions originate, sex may be variously construed as a sheer physiological function; as an invention of the Devil; as a moral duty to preserve the race (overlooking the fact that the more dutiful we are in this area, the greater the problems of preservation become); as a shameful marital obligation; as a therapeutic measure; as a mystery, a punishment, a privilege, a reward, a weapon, an obscenity, a thing of beauty, or a nuisance. That sex can be pleasure—that sex *should* be pleasure—is a concept that seemingly was wiped off the face of the earth beginning in the year 1800, a year that began according to the Danish sexual historian Poul Henningson, "the only respectable century in the history of mankind."

For two thousand odd years before the Victorian era, sex was something to be enjoyed. The morality of ancient Greece, fountainhead of Western culture, emphasized delight in love. Its very gods showed the way. Few pantheons can match the immortals of Olympus for romantic abandon, emotional involvements, and just plain sexual enthusiasm. Pleasure was the very name given to the beautiful-beyond-compare daughter of Cupid and Psyche. Father Zeus himself set the Olympian tone, being willing (and fortunately able) to go to any lengths and forms to enjoy the latest object of his august ardor. The only showers of gold one encounters nowadays in the arenas of love are likely to be the one expended in the effort to conquer a woman, and the subsequent one, in the form of alimony, necessary to get rid of her.

Much of our attitude toward sex today seems based on the opposite determination—not only to prevent others from enjoying it, but to see that we get as little pleasure as possible out of it ourselves. "One could speculate," writes Nelson Foote in his essay, *Sex as Play*, "whether it is the puritan tendency to frown upon play, or the puritan tradition that sex is intrinsically sinful, or both in combination, which still obscure and confuse the significance of the manifest situation. As our advertisers imply daily in a thousand ways, the attractions of sex make it the favorite form of play for millions of Americans. Why do not our thinkers go on from there to contemplate the kind of social life which might result from formal recognition of this fact? Is it because to grant its status as play is felt to legitimize its pursuit without restraint? If so, the thinker does not understand the nature of play."

The nature of play, you will recall, according to the three characteristics formulated for it by Johan Huizinga, is this: it is a voluntary activity; it is something that takes place not in "real life" but in a sphere of activity with an emotional connotation of its own; and, finally, it has definite limits of time and place. It is, in Huizinga's words, "a temporary world within the ordinary world, dedicated to the performance of an act apart . . . Into the confusion of life it brings a temporary, a limited perfection."

Neither the romantic poet, the physiologist, nor the sociologist could quarrel very well with those phrases as a definition of love and sex. Certainly love and sex are voluntary activities that carry a man and woman, for a brief time, into a world and an act apart. The "real" world disappears; indeed, at the moment of culmination consciousness itself narrows to a focus on one brief, blinding point of existence, a temporary perfection. *Post coitum omne animal triste est* is the propaganda of neurotics.

But the scientists and the salesmen of sex have gone a long way toward spoiling these temporary perfections. Lovers are now so busily concerned with technique that they are mistaking the means of sex for the ends.

Alfred C. Kinsey, the first investigator of love and sex to turn them into a typesetter's nightmare, was also one of the first formally to recognize the pleasureable aspect of sex. "There is no doubt," he writes, as if it were news, "that coitus . . . may serve as a source of pleasure for one or both of the individuals involved." Yet at the same time Kinsey, by reducing sex to a series of statistical tables, brought to a head the growing "scientification" of love that now afflicts the middle and the upper classes. (We may dispense with the lower classes for two reasons: 1. sociologists assure us members of the lower class are characteristically crude in their approach to sex, indulging in it perfunctorily, brusquely, clumsily, and unimaginatively; 2. sociologists also assure us this is of no import, since there are no longer any Americans in the lower class.)

"Kinsey certainly took sex out of the rosy realm of the bees and the flowers," a marriage counselor observed. "But I wonder if he didn't go too far in the other direction. We have exchanged the pleasure of sex for the measure of sex. It's now more like a game of football: we are so busy counting the number of yards to a first down that we don't have time to study the formations or to enjoy the plays."

The pleasures of sex are being diluted, if not drowned, by its alleged intricacies. There is today not only the question of whether a woman has had an orgasm (the technicians' *sine qua non* of female pleasure in sex), but of which particular section of her anatomy was responsible. There are questions of frequency, timing, style, position, and the quality of the preliminary skirmishing. The mass media are filled each month with such matters. The best-seller lists are studded with marriage manuals that are to the pleasures of sex what the automotive mechanics' handbook is to the pleasures of motoring.

In *The Sexual Behavior of the Human Female,* for instance, there are 179 statistical tables and 155 charts and graphs clinically pinpointing every facet of the sex relationship, from the heart rate during orgasm to the correlation between religion and petting techniques. Kinsey—and the equally technical-minded researchers who have followed him—measured sexual fulfillment in terms of a person's age, education, father's occupation, and a host of allegedly related factors. But not once do they attempt to measure or even to discuss sex in terms of tenderness, affection, or enjoyment. Although there are more than four thousand separate subject listings in the index of *Human Female,* the words "love," "enjoyment," or "pleasure" do not appear at all.

True, Ovid wrote a marriage manual a couple of millennia ago, but it was concerned not so much with the techniques of love as with the arts of love. Its aim was not so much to enable a man and woman to perform proficiently as to enable them to enjoy what they were doing. In sex, as in writing or politics, a little proficiency goes a long way.

The effect of the precisionist approach to sexual love is to remove from it the elements of pleasure. Can one imagine Pantagruel, say, pausing in one of his lusty tumbling matches to inquire of his partner what point she had reached in her sex-response curve? Is it conceivable that Tristan and Isolde would have called the whole thing off because of a difference in timing? Would the virginal Sir Galahad have sacrificed his purity on the altar of peer-group conformity in order to be a regular knight?

Yet things very much like these—and just as ridiculous— are happening today. Marriage counselors report an upsurge of women clients who complain that their husbands are unable to bring them to a satisfactory sexual climax. They are saying in effect: "Don't get me wrong, I love my husband; but it isn't like the book says it should be." Couples who enjoyed sex before they started analyzing it are now unable to find any pleasure in it.

At a Southern university not long ago a male student proudly admitted that he went "all the way" with as many girls as he could.

"Do you think this is wise in terms of your future marital happiness?" he was asked.

"Not exactly," he said.

"Well, do you get a great deal of pleasure out of these conquests?"

"Not particularly," the youth said. "But look, according to studies I've read, more than half the fellows in the country have premarital intercourse. And I'm nineteen—right at the peak of my sexual drive, they say."

Recent studies of the emotional relationships between the sexes on college campuses show an increasing tendency to conform to group standards. Premarital intercourse, which one might think would be indulged in for reasons of purely personal enjoyment, is a function more of status than of pleasure.

Studies based on depth interviews with thousands of men and women students reveal the existence of specific codes of sexual behavior based not on morality but on rank and caste. One goes to such a point with a girl of superior social status, further with a girl of equal social status, and all the way, if possible, with a girl of lower social status. Similar codes exist for girls, though in reverse. The consistent moral is that a person's actions do not spring so much out of his own desires or standards as out of what is considered to be proper under the campus codes. One does not seek pleasure for one's own sake, but in order to conform. Not long ago the authorities at a Midwestern college announced that coeds could stay out an additional hour on Saturday nights. The students—male and female—yelled blue murder. "We'll just have to hang around the dormitory steps smooching for an extra hour," despaired one young man, "because those girls would rather die than be caught going inside even a minute before curfew. The fellow who doesn't keep his date out to the very last moment is going to be a dead duck."

This depersonalization of sex often begins in the early stages of sex education, where some educators view the whole problem as one of terminology alone. One school system reports that early-grade pupils are first made acquainted with sex in their spelling classes. Spelling lessons include, as a matter of course, the technical words for various sexual organs and functions. Of this, Fritz Redl, an expert in sex education, has said:

"If, they think, you only give the children the 'pure' terms of scientific language, then you have done all that is needed. They try to de-emotionalize sex for them, to make a valuable piece of scientific insight out of what was a fantasy before. They think they have separated sex knowledge from all emotional content, and feel very pleased about it. I do not doubt the effect of moral satisfaction this has for the adult, but I think that a simple mental hygiene consideration will show us how wrong it is. . . ."

Sex is being "de-emotionalized" at virtually every age level. The first fumbling boy-girl relationships of earlier generations were filled, no doubt, with moments of embarrassment or confusion. But they were also filled with moments of discovery and of joy. There was an opportunity to find out for yourself—at your own pace—what the opposite sex was all about. Today, youngsters are paired off while they are still in elementary school. Girls and boys need partners for the dancing class, and "proms" take place as early as the fourth grade. Boys of eleven in miniature dinner jackets, and girls of eleven in décolleté ball gowns and false-filled bras are matched by their teachers or parents with due regard for the families' social and financial status. Preadolescents are encouraged to "steady-date" by mothers who fear their children won't be popular.

The arid artificialities of these early ventures into the world of male and female carry over into the age of puberty. The emotional lives of today's teenagers are built around a pattern resembling the sterile complexities of an involved but essentially meaningless ritual. The forms are there—the dating, the petting, the pinning—but the emotional foundation is missing. The youngsters are social insects, going about their appointed sexual rounds and fulfilling their appointed sexual functions like termites, without any emotional or intellectual understanding of what they are doing, or why.

In my youth a date was occasionally an interesting experience. Every so often you went out with a new girl, you talked about new things (or old things in a new way). You went to different places with different people. And you never knew exactly what might happen when you took her home. Not so now. The young people I know cling to their "steadies" like drowning swimmers clutching at planks. They run with the same crowd, to the same places. They talk about the same things, listen to the same records—or different records that sound the same. And they know exactly how far they will get—or go—because they reached that same point last week. As a matter of fact, they reached the same point on their first or second date, because the peer group had set the permissible boundaries.

There are basic qualitative and quantitative criteria for romance. Many girls actually have schedules for the amount, duration, and type of kisses they will grant, depending on whom their date is. Other young people, taking their cue from the proliferating research that is codifying sexual behavior, proceed in "stages"—cold-bloodedly moving from Stages A and B up to Stage F. The imprimatur of social science has established that certain stages are permissible—indeed proper —with certain persons at certain times. There is no exploration, no risk—and therefore not much reward.

It may be the desperate search for this reward—which youth instinctively knows should exist—that is the cause today of the ever-growing rate of teenage marriages. But even here pleasure is absent. Do you read the newspaper and magazine stories about these young-old husbands and wives? They live, usually, in depressing little apartments or trailers or Quonset huts, worrying about money or babies or in-laws, already beginning to be bored with each other and to resent their loss of freedom. At seventeen or eighteen or nineteen they are solemn and sober and joyless, like those unfortunate babies with wizened faces who are born ancient.

By separating emotion from knowledge, the centrifuge of social science goes a long way toward contributing to the decline of pleasure in romance. But another large part of the job is accomplished by cheapening the emotions that remain;

by turning love and sex into commercialized obscenity compounded equally of Brigitte Bardot and Baron Richard von Krafft-Ebing.

The indictment is too familiar to be labored long here. The point is simply that even the *search* for sexual substitutes, for vicarious romance, is rendered as sterile as the real thing by the *café brûlot* of improbable passions and unlikely delights that grace—or, if you will, dis-grace—the semi-pornographic magazines and the clinically oversexed best-sellers that comprise a hugh part of our reading matter.

The greatest offender of all, of course, is that factory of shoddy illusion, Hollywood, where romantic pleasures are distorted to the weird perspectives of the box office. If the theoretical man from Mars were to base a sexual analysis of the American people on nothing but what he could see in our movies, he could scarcely be blamed for reporting us a nation of exhibitionists, voyeurs, seducers, rapists, homosexuals, nymphomaniacs, prostitutes, frigid wives, impotent husbands, and—at best—coy young men and women who play teasingly at adolescent versions of the male-female relationship. Only once in a great while would our Martian find a picture in which the hero and heroine enjoy normal sexual appetites, and satisfy them normally. One reason is, of course, that normal sexual pleasures have a hard time getting by Hollywood's self-censorship code. It is perfectly permissible to show call girls, pregnant adolescents, adulterers, or necrophiles. It is forbidden to convey the information that a married couple make love to each other.

The main reason Hollywood makes sex distasteful rather than pleasurable is that it suffers from the basic American misconception that there is some mystical difference between love and sex. The "sexy" girl cannot also be a "good" girl; at least, not at the same time. The dichotomy can be illustrated by a line of dialogue spoken by the heel-hero of John O'Hara's *Butterfield* 8. He has spent the last several reels making love with Elizabeth Taylor. She finally realizes it is wrong to come between a man and wife, renounces her lover, and is killed in an automobile crash to satisfy the vengeance requirements of the Production Code which, unlike God, requires sinners to be punished even if they repent. At any rate, talking of the deceased Liz, the hero says solemnly to his wife, "On the outside she was all sex . . . but inside she was struggling for respectability."

If one draws this artificial line between sacred and profane love, between the good girl and the sexy girl, as Hollywood does draw it, then obviously the sex portrayed is bound to be devoid of the positive emotions and bereft of the positive pleasures.

Seldom does a psychoanalyst impale a problem in a pithy paragraph, but Theodore Reik has managed to do so in his analysis of the decline of sexual pleasure in America:

"The expression 'to have fun' becomes in America more and more synonymous with having sexual intercourse," he writes. "This new connotation is symptomatic of the emotional degradation of the sexual process. Sexual experience is in reality very serious, and sometimes even tragic. If it's only 'fun,' it is not even funny any longer."

The fact of the matter is that we do not feast our senses at all any more. We play it safe, and we like it that way. We take what is given to us, and we are secretly glad it is all as passionless as it is. We go forth into the sensory world halfheartedly, protected against its pagan touches by gloves, dark glasses, heavy clothes, thick shoes; even our flesh is sani-sealed against life by coatings of anti-perspirants and cosmetics.

We should wander the streets of the world gaily caparisoned and searching for adventures of the senses. Instead we walk our daily tightropes blinkered and Saran-wrapped, hoping to Heaven that nothing will happen.

Chapter IX

SOME MASKS OF PLEASURE

Think of this, good peers, But as a thing of custom: 'tis no other; Only it spoils the pleasure of the time.

—SHAKESPEARE, *Macbeth*

RANKING among the most catholic of American pleasures is gardening. It is indulged in by both sexes, by all ages, by rich and poor, by the educated as well as the ignorant, by homeowners and home-renters in all sections of the country. Only apartment dwellers without snake plants are exempt. All told, 50,000,000 of us spend more than one billion dollars a year in a frenzy of green-thumbing.

From this, it might be safe to assume that most, if not all, of these people enjoy working in their gardens. But a field reconnaissance conducted a few years ago by the Center for the Study of Leisure gave evidence that fewer than half of all gardeners like gardening. Worse yet, those who do not get pleasure out of it are either unaware of their feelings or are camouflaging them. For example, when they were asked the direct question: Do you enjoy gardening? five out of six persons answered, "Yes." But when these same people were asked to name the things they took pleasure in doing, more than half never even mentioned gardening.

The possibility still existed that some of these tillers of the soil might originally have been enthusiastic but had lost interest as a result of the depredations of weeds, aphids, drought, Japanese beetles, and other destroyers of flora. The researchers therefore refined their study, limiting it now to gardeners who devoted the most time and effort to lawn and flower bed, and who were rewarded most lushly. But, again, only a small percentage even of these successful gardeners said they got any pleasure out of their endeavors.

Why, then, do so many people work so hard at gardening?

"The inference is unhappily inescapable," says sociologist Reuel Denney, "that most people do their gardening as a chore whose chief reward is the achievement of status—a conclusion borne out by the fact that, unlike the European grounds, the United States garden is not out back, where it can be enjoyed with a maximum of privacy, but out front, where the neighbors can see it."

In this wise, the American garden is a cultural cognate of the Trobiand Island yam-house. A Trobriander builds his yam storage hut in such a way that passers-by can estimate how many yams are inside it. There are wide gaps between the beams so that one may see the quality of the fruit; of course the best yams are placed up forward. Especially excellent yams are decorated and hung up outside the hut. But the chief of a Trobriand village need not go to these lengths. His position is established regardless of the size of his yams. Similarly, an American whose prestige derives from more secure foundations can afford to ignore or even flaunt the community lawn-and-garden standards. Not long ago, for instance, missile scientist Wernher von Braun, whose professional achievements afford him all the distinction he can want, bought a house and promptly poured a thick layer of grass-green concrete over the front yard—probably gaining, in the process, even more esteem than if he had chosen to raise rare plants.

It was of course Thorstein Veblen who observed that people are torn between choosing pleasures for their own sake, or for the purpose of maintaining and upgrading their social position. The American thirst for status and its symbols has been sufficiently documented to need no belaboring here. It has reached what is probably its high-water mark: a radiation fallout shelter is now available with lounge chairs and wall-to-wall carpeting as well as the usual paraphernalia of sledge hammers and first-aid kits. You can be the first family on your block to wait out the H-bomb in luxury.

Social security in the emotional sense once rested on the double base of a man's identification with his work and of his place in an integrated family unit. As both of these supports eroded, a man's repute came to depend on fragments of his life: where (or whether) he works; how much he earns; where he lives; his wife's appearance; the car he drives, and so on. But these existent badges of wordly success are becoming outmoded. Social distinctions currently in vogue are already blurring. Few neighborhoods, for example, are any longer truly exclusive. An architecturally tricked-up twenty-thousand-dollar house may seem more elaborate, from the outside, than a conservative fifty-thousand-dollar house. The car one drives today has little to do with the income one earns. Higher education is a universal privilege; the country teems with college graduates. Custom-tailored suits and couturier gowns are mass-produced at popular prices with virtually unnoticeable changes from the costly originals. And the chaste diamond ring and simple pearl necklace pale alongside coruscating costume jewelry.

New badges of success are needed to establish rank in our superficially equalitarian society. And a convenient area of life in which they can be acquired and displayed is the realm of pleasure.

There is nothing unnatural about this. When we are all

members of the leisure class, status becomes a matter not of
having time to spare but of the uses we make of that time.
The American whose primary concern is to move up to a
higher ranking in his work, his house, his car, is logically going to adopt as well what he considers "upper class" pleasures.
(If he cannot adopt them he will adapt them. One culturally
hep inventor recently patented a device which, bolted to the
transom of a plain old rowboat equipped with a five-horse-
power outboard, will scoop up such an impressive stream of
water that others on the lake will mistake the rowboat for a
hydroplane. On a less imaginative level are the synthetic sun-
tanning preparations on the market. Don't let the neighbors
know you can't send the family away for the summer! Coat
them all with a tannic-acid solution and look as if you'd all
been in Hawaii!)

"In our leisure we stand exposed," writes social analyst Max
Kaplan. "What we do, whether on the noblest of levels and
aspirations or the lowest of tastes, is a clue or indication of
what we are, *who* we are, *where* we want to go." It should
come as no surprise, then, that under these circumstances external standards rather than internal wants—social pressures
rather than personal appetites—tend to dominate our choice
of pleasures; to dress them in masks; and to pervert them to
ends far removed from their original goals. Gardening is a
prime example of this. Labeled a recreation, it is undertaken,
as we have seen, less for the sake of enjoyment than for the
sake of two of the principal masks of pleasure—esteem and
conformity.

In the absence of clear-cut personal desires, conformity accounts for a large slice of the pleasure pie. If on a summer
weekend you could hover over America in one of the new
satellites that carries a telescopic camera eye, you would see
millions of people engaged in pastimes—building patios, cooking on backyard barbecues, taking home movies, driving on

jammed highways—not so much because they enjoy them as because everyone else is doing them too. So they must be fun, mustn't they? Or, if not fun, at least socially acceptable.

In one Eastern city, for example, almost all lawyers of any standing or aspirations take a Florida vacation in the winter; it has come to be virtually a requirement for professional prestige. The barrister who prefers to ski is simply out of luck.

Conforming to a pleasure pattern may also be the means of entree to a particular group, for cliques clump together around specific amusements—the boating "crowd," the golfing "crowd." The man who chooses a cigarette brand because virile cowboys smoke it is just as likely to choose a pastime because it has been adopted by his social demigod or by his coterie of friends. (Birds of a pleasure flock togethure.) These motivations are well known to the merchandisers of recreation. The makers of sports cars and adult games, for instance, know their best bet for commercial success is to sell first the social or intellectual leaders in a community; the climbers will follow.

But many Americans go along with fashions in pleasure out of sheer sociability. Even card-playing, which ranks with television and movie-going as a major leisure-time activity, seems to be rooted in the national need to be part of a great big happy activity group. Sociologist Irving Crespi, fascinated by figures that showed Americans buy one hundred million decks of cards a year, and that 57 per cent of us play cards more or less regularly, ran a survey to find out why. Ten per cent of his respondents said card-playing was their favorite diversion, and another 22 per cent said they liked it very much. But 41 per cent were lukewarm; card-playing is "nice," they agreed, yet they could take it or leave it. Sixteen per cent played cards because they had nothing else to do. Eleven per cent of the card-players did not enjoy it at all. Strangely, those who play cards the most are the ones who relish it the least!

The majority of people who play cards routinely once a week or oftener make up the bulk of those who dislike the game. Interviews shed some light on the contradiction. For a few people, Crespi found, card-playing is a means of access to status—the bridge party at the "right" home, the poker game with "men who count." But, for most, card-playing is a "universal social solvent"—the simplest, safest, easiest way to solve the problem of passing time. It serves as a neutral focal point for a neighborhood group; it acts as a substitute for conversation; it offers a nearly hypnotic ritual; and it relieves one of all social demands except to ante up or follow suit.

"No man," said Samuel Johnson, "is a hypocrite in his pleasures." But the good doctor was wrong. Builders of residential swimming pools have noted that a surprising number of people who have pools installed cannot swim. Many a suburban family joins an expensive country club merely to prove it can afford the substantial fee. Many an insurance salesman who would prefer to be at the ball game can be found on the golf course, making contacts. There is even a legend about the man who, in public, drank nothing but champagne; he hated the taste, but it was wonderful for his status. The hypocrisy works in reverse, too. Some people who would secretly like to watch television programs refuse to have a set in their home so they can bask in the glory of being considered eggheads. Researchers who make recreation surveys report that the answers most people give to questions about their leisure activities are usually false: "They say they do the things they think they ought to be doing, or things that are prestigious, like chess and horseback riding."

The upsurge of recondite pleasures—spelunking, wine expertising, sports car rally racing, skin diving, sky diving—is attributable in large part to their ability to gratify status claims. Yet these and other esoteric amusements deserve less the name of pleasures than of fads. The proof of a pleasure is its staying power. The proof of a fad is its volatility, the swiftness with which it appears and vanishes. Characteristically, too, the fad catches hold at first within a small group; when it passes to the masses, the group remains intact and ready to glorify the next fad. The same people—or, to be more exact, the same kind of people, for in this area age takes its toll—who were clambering down into bat-infested caves a few years ago, when spelunking was the thing to do, are now snorkeling.

Nor is it merely *what* people do for pleasure that confers status. It is also to a great degree *how* and *where* and *when* and *with whom* they do it. There is clearly a difference between swimming at Coney Island and at Palm Beach. The winter vacationist is a cut above the summer one. It is pointless, in terms of status, to keep going to Florida or Mexico when all one's friends are going to Aruba or Tahiti. Even such a homely pleasure as belonging to a club or lodge (80,000,000 of us belong to two million voluntary organizations) is fraught with status possibilities. One night a week the store clerk becomes a "president," the housewife a "corresponding secretary." Each is conscious of the privileges and perquisites of his unaccustomed role. The non-office-holding member gets his sense of importance in the group's discussions and decisions; when he votes, he exercises power. It was not entirely laughable, for example, when the late Helen Hokinson drew a *New Yorker* cartoon in which a solemn-faced club president asked the assembled ladies, "But do the members of the Westchester Garden Clubs *want* a free Yugoslavia?"

At the same time, there are a growing number of Americans who say they find pleasure in discussing exactly such matters as the future of Yugoslavia, existentialism, documentary film classics, and other aspects of Culture. This "cultural explosion" has been well documented. To reprise the evidence, there are at latest count thirty-five major, 140 secondary, and over a thousand community symphony orchestras in the country; attendance at concerts has more than doubled in the past twenty years; classical and operatic recordings account for the bulk of nearly half a billion dollars' worth of record sales; live opera and ballet performances are sold out weeks in advance; attendance at art galleries and museums has multiplied—New York's Metropolitan Museum of Art had more than 4,000,000 visitors last year; adult education classes are bursting at the seams; agitation increases for "good" television programs; a million paperback books are printed every day, and the number of hard-cover books published grows each year.

What does all this add up to if not a flowering of the intellectual desert where once skulked only the Babbitts and the booboisie? On the surface, we are living in the midst of a new Renaissance. But this resurgence of the Golden Age does not stand up quite so well under closer scrutiny. One is reminded of Stanley Hyman's application of the Law of Raspberry Jam to the "cultural explosion": the wider you spread it, the thinner it gets.

It is true, for example, that the 4,000,000 people who annually visit the Metropolitan Museum *are* more than twice as many as attend an entire year's schedule of athletic events at Madison Square Garden. But the operators of this cultural numbers racket overlook one point: admission to the Metropolitan is free; to get into the Garden costs money. Moreover, "to visit an art gallery is, undoubtedly, to participate to some extent" in art, as Gerald Johnson has observed. But, he goes on to say, "it is nothing like as deep a participation as to have visited the same gallery occasionally for 20 years, to have noted its new acquisitions . . . in short to have acquired a proprietary interest in the place."

It is true, also, that more books than ever are being published; but reading is not among our most passionate pleasures. Millions of us do not read a single hard-cover book a year for the sheer enjoyment of it. At any given time only three out of twenty of us are reading a book of any kind, compared with eleven out of twenty Englishmen. Paperback publishers have been putting out abstruse volumes and long-neglected (often for good reason) classics which find their place on coffee tables and downstairs bookshelves; but what *is* read by these millions that were mentioned is Erle Stanley Gardner, Grace Metalious, and anything with a nearly naked girl on the cover. Dr. W. Oliver Martin, a professor of philosophy, told a conference on leisure about an advertisement he saw for a paperback edition of Plato:

"Part of the description was a suggestion on how to use it. Since it did not cost very much, you could tear out two or three pages each morning and you would not lose a lot of money. By reading it on your way to work, it would be fresh in your mind. Then, what you were supposed to do was to drop a few words to your boss, like, 'As Plato said . . .' Now, there is a use of leisure time! Here is bringing culture to the people!"

Movies? The seriously good ones usually lose money. The Westerns, the horror films, and the spectaculars, most of them run-of-the-mill and an insult to intelligence, make millions.

Music? "They will tell you," says musicologist Ernst Bacon, "how the radio (and recordings) has caused millions to know the *Unfinished* and the *Eroica* symphonies. But how *do* they know them? Mostly as dinner music, music to which to talk, argue, buy, sell, or read newspapers. It is bad enough to din trivial music into our ears all day long. It is worse to use the masterpieces for this purpose."

Television? Comment unnecessary, but for the record it can be pointed out that of a hundred pilot films being considered for the 1962–63 season, action-adventure, situation comedy, and animated cartoons comprised about 85 per cent.

Personal taste is giving ground to packaged taste in the form of record clubs, book clubs, art portfolio clubs, sculpture-of-the-month clubs, theater parties, magazines of culture. Our very history is crammed into a pleasure package (and shamefully betrayed) in New York City's Freedomland, a brassy amusement park laid out in the geographic shape of America, and which features carnival attractions synthetically linked to the nation's physical features and traditional events. Not long ago some Hollywood showmen announced plans for "Bible Storyland": visitors were going to be able to eat in "Babylon" at the "Hanging Gardens Restaurant," get married in Solomon's Temple, see an animated figure of Joseph working in a carpenter's shop, and ride glass-bottomed boats over the "Dead Sea" to look at "Sodom and Gomorrah." Nothing more has been heard of this proposal since a group of clergymen denounced it as blasphemy.

We are in, I should induce from the foregoing, an era not of culture but of Instant Culture. It is not up to the natural flavor or quality by any means, but it is much more convenient and highly attractive as a mask for pleasure.

Victor Ratner, a magazine editor, in an essay defending television program content on the grounds of the "fifth free-dom—freedom of taste," made the point that "culturally speaking, we now live on a public highway . . . culture invades the privacy of one's home . . . most of the cultural product is not designed for an aristocracy, but for the appreciation, the standards and uses of masses of people." This is substantially true, and a key point. Discretionary time and money are now distributed in America on a democratic bell curve. The bulk of both belongs to the middle and the lower middle classes. Pleasures—including cultural ones—are being shaped more and more to their taste. We find it more logical, for example, to build fast cars and good roads to carry many people to already crowded vacation areas than we do to preserve the solitude of a wilderness region that might be accessible only to a relative few. We produce portable radios and phonographs in profusion, but virtually no listenable music. Bond issues to raise money for baseball stadia are passed by whopping majorities, but raising tax money for better public library service is culture of another color.

The general assumption is that if we are truly our own masters in any area of life, it is in the pleasures that we choose. But this sanguine theory reckons without the fact that our enjoyments, like our duties, come under compulsions that bear little relation to pleasure; and wear disguises that more often fool the actor than the audience.

Perhaps it takes a more autocratic character than most Americans possess to be unmasked about our pleasures. Such as, for example, a former Shah of Iran who, on a state visit to England, declined an invitation to see the races at Ascot.

"I am well aware," said the Shah, "that some horses run faster than others."

Chapter X

THE TRIALS OF TRAVEL

All the world is sad and dreary, everywhere I roam . . .

—STEPHEN FOSTER

OUT WEST, where trains are trains and not the palsied excuses for transportation they have become in the effete East, some travelers still ride them for pleasure. Streamliners are equipped with Vista-Dome, Scenic-Dome, or some similar double-dome car through whose transparent bubble top passengers can view the wonders of nature. Even the limitations imposed by a rigid right-of-way have been partially overcome. Not able to detour at will to a point of interest as an automobile can; or as an airplane can make a low pass or two over Grand Canyon on its way to the Coast, the transcontinental rail lines ingeniously arrange to bring an occasional point of interest to the right-of-way. Thus the Santa Fe Railroad, for example, advertises a "Ten Minute Stopover in the Old World":

"One of the high points of a Super Chief trip comes at Albuquerque, New Mexico. Because here the train stops to let you spend ten minutes in the picturesque world of Spanish Conquistadores and Indians. You'll see amazing things. Meet fascinating people. Relive history. And you do it all in ten minutes. . . ."

Anyone who has spent these ten minutes at the railroad station in Albuquerque may well remember them as ten of the most dispiriting minutes of his life. This "picturesque world" is largely a tawdry mixture of gimcrack jewelry, imitation kachina dolls, and Indian blankets hawked by stage Indians in an atmosphere about as spontaneous as that of a Hollywood film set during the tenth take of a scene. The passengers self-consciously walk up and down the station platform and look at the Indians and finger the blankets and perhaps buy a pair of stereotyped silver and turquoise earrings. Some may feel disappointed; some, empathetically embarrassed at the sight of the noble red men working as a concessionaire's shill. But when the ten minutes are up and their train pulls out, many of these travelers manage to convince themselves, against the evidence of their senses, that they have indeed seen amazing things and met fascinating people.

It is reasonable to ask how even the least sensitive person can delude himself about the gulf between the promise and the reality. The answer, it seems to me, comes in two parts.

One is the corruption of the private vision by the standardized illusion.

Mass communication has resulted in the creation of mass images. For instance, the young man who daydreams of future fame and fortune once had a large selection of models to choose from. Today he is most likely to see himself in his mind's eye as that archetype of success, the captain of industry—a die-cut cardboard character who negligently studies the stock ticker in his club while a deferent waiter proffers, on silver tray, a glass of impeccably aristocratic bourbon. In like manner the young woman who wants to picture herself as a glamour girl takes the mental short cut of identifying with whichever movie actress or international celebrity is currently popular.

The dreamer's dream has been dreamed for him. He settles, often without realizing it, for the standard vision that has been dinned into his subconscious by the mass media.

"This kind of borrowing," a commentator noted, "is to be seen in all areas of dreaming today. A woman dreaming of something practical, like a new kitchen, usually doesn't imagine one custom-designed by herself. She selects one of the numerous images of new kitchens already made available. Likewise, the man who dreams of escape—and this is an especially deplorable example—conjures up standardized versions of how to get away from it all. The would-be escaper today may start to form an image of a deserted South Sea island. But soon travel-folder versions of How To Escape enter his mind . . . Into his visions slide the projections of luxury accommodations in the wilderness. . . ."

The science of optics gives us the phenomenon of the after-image. If you look at a bright electric light and then quickly shift your gaze to a neutral background, you will still see, for a few seconds, the ghost image of the shining bulb. So it is with the traveler. Dazzled by the brilliance of the synthetic image, he tends to keep on seeing it even when it isn't there.

In other words, the pleasure traveler in these days of fierce competition for the tourist dollar has been brainwashed.

Or eyewashed.

He sees not what is actually in front of him, but what he has been told he *will* see, or *should* see. Thus, the visitor to the French Riviera, even while he is actually looking at a real beach—generally a narrow and pebbly strip of black sand—emotionally gazes at an after-image of a broad white beach which—in the advertisements—lines the Mediterranean coast. And he who spends ten minutes at the Albuquerque station sees noble red men and conquistadores in a picturesque world.

The second part of the answer to the pleasure traveler's acceptance of what he knows to be essentially illusory lies in the self-deception he practices to assure himself that he is enjoying himself. For he cannot emotionally afford to admit that he isn't.

"Vacations," a British essayist once said, "are less a time of enjoyment than a time of general consent to be bored under a hollow show of enjoyment. The best hope for many of us is that, by pretending very hard, the pretense may come to have a sort of secondary reality."

The necessity to enjoy is nowhere so imperative as on a trip. The average tourist is spending time and money that have been both hard-earned; also, he will not in all likelihood pass this way again. And so nothing—not even the facts—must interfere.

Nowadays, both the necessity and the pretense are in crescendo. Millions of Americans prowl the world each year. According to the American Society of Travel Agents, 100,000,-000 of us spent over sixteen billion dollars on jaunts within the United States last year. Another 2,000,000 people spent two and a half billion dollars on travel overseas.

"Travel has come of age as a significant human activity," proudly declares William D. Patterson, an expert on tourism. "On the level of cultural, economic and political intercourse among nations and peoples, travel takes its rightful place beside diplomacy, trade and communications as part of the twentieth century's resources in civilization's terrifying race with catastrophe." (The average tourist, however, blissfully unaware of his civilizing influence on world affairs, is usually more concerned about his race with his private catastrophe—which is that the last room in town will be rented by the time he reaches his night's destination.)

As a matter of fact, one of the main reasons for the loss of pleasure in pleasure travel is that travel *has* "come of age

as a significant human activity"—or, at least, has been so labeled. It is, therefore, no longer guiltlessly to be enjoyed for
its own sake. A motivation research organization recently ques-
tioned a group of travelers and a group of prospective travelers
to Europe as to why they had made, or wanted to make, the
trip. Significantly, the answers emphasized the cultural and
educational benefits: to learn how people in other countries
live, to see some particular historical or artistic sights, to get
a background for the understanding of world affairs.

In fulfillment of these avowed aims the tourist, fat with
maps and guidebooks, debouches from his hotel each morning to begin his rounds. His day passes—indeed, his days pass
—in dutiful peregrinations from church to museum to palace
to the town hall. The gabble of his guide can scarcely be
heard over the competing gabble of the guides just ahead and
just behind. In *The World of Venice* James Morris writes
about the tourists who come to Italy's Fort Lauderdale; but
what he says applies equally well to all tourists who take their
cultural motivations seriously: "The truth is that most visitors
move among her wonders mindlessly, pumped briskly through
the machine and spewed out along the causeway as soon as
they are properly processed."

What makes the picture truly pathetic is that most travelers do not, *au fond*, wish to spend their time this way at all.

Motivation researchers learned this when they asked the
same panels the same question—but this time they asked the
groups to suggest reasons why their *friends or neighbors* might
want to go to Europe. In the language of social research this
is a "projective" query. By answering for a hypothetical third
person the respondent has little reason to fear he will reveal
some embarrassing desire or interest of his own; yet at the
same time the answers he gives reflect his own feelings more
accurately, in most cases, than do his replies to a direct question.

"When he is talking about *his* reasons for travel to Europe, the traveler tends to play down pleasure, play up education," reported the researchers. "But responses to projective questions show that the real balance of motivations is somewhat less on learning, more on enjoying, than the traveler would have you (or himself) believe."

Specifically, persons who said *they* traveled primarily for culture and education saw these motives as considerably less important for other people. The motives of these others, the panelists said, ran more to getting away from routine, having fun, and enjoying the night life. "It is well within the bounds of the interpretation of this kind of question," say the researchers, "to infer that the change of scenery and the pleasures of the flesh are potent incentives to travelers as well as to their neighbors . . . The wish for a good time is a strong—although guardedly expressed—motive for travel. People want some fun along with the education, but they do not seem to want to ask for this fun too loudly."

Since one of the rationales of this study was to aid travel advertisers to appeal more successfully to potential customers, the researchers had this suggestion to make for walking the pleasure-culture tightrope:

"Merchandise culture and education in an atmosphere which clearly communicates the fact that travel has its elements of fun . . . When both culture and pleasure can be conveyed at the same time in the same advertisement, the appeal will be stronger than if either one is featured without the other. Just to illustrate this point, the picture in a travel advertisement might show man and wife studying a monument or other cultural artifact while a kiosk in the background displays a poster of can-can girls . . . A cartoon might show the wife studying her guidebook while she walks down the street while the husband is momentarily distracted by a shapely leg."

"For my part," Robert Louis Stevenson wrote, "I travel not to go anywhere, but to go. I travel for travel's sake. The great affair is to move."

Certainly, travelers move today. But not the way Stevenson meant. From seventy miles an hour on the superhighways to seven hundred miles an hour in the jet streams, we pile up mileage avidly, as if it were proof of some mysterious superiority. Like the Persian messengers cited by Herodotus, our velocity is unhuman. Where we went or what we did seems to be not half so important as how far we went. Breathes there the man with soul so dead who never to his fellow hath said, "Yes, sir, we did five thousand miles in three weeks?"

The man who spends his vacation in one place is a vanishing species. In his stead we have the nomad, seeking pleasure in a series of one-night stands. This urgent wanderlust is even more apparent in the overseas than in the domestic traveler. His chief objective is to touch base in as many different countries as will squeeze into his itinerary. The airlines are cognizant of this passion to work up a lengthy list of "I've been there" places. They concentrate on pointing out how many stopovers can be made in different nations for the price of one round-trip ticket. "Ten countries . . . twenty-five cities!" says the ad. Presumably it does not matter to the traveler *which* cities. He is out to rack up a score, and Amsterdam serves as well as Vienna, or vice versa.

In truth, it makes little difference to the country-collector which city he is seeing. He is usually so ill-prepared in knowledge about it, so briefly there, and so anxious to get on to the next stop that he skims across its surface like a water strider on a pond. One is tempted to pass off as exaggerations the tales of tourists who wake in their hotel in the morning and cannot remember which city they are in. But I actually saw and heard the meeting, on the steps of the Acropolis in Athens, of two American couples who evidently had been running into each other all over Europe and the Middle East. They exchanged smiles of greeting and tried to place their most recent encounter. Finally one of the women gave up. Sweetly she asked, "What *was* the name of that country we saw you in last week?"

But unlike Robert Louis Stevenson, the mileage-maniac and the nation-collector are not on the go simply for pleasure's sake. They are on the go for, among other things, status. Not too many years ago one could acquire enough status to last a lifetime merely by making a trip to England. But with jet planes hurtling to the farthest reaches, going to England now is about as prestigious as going to the corner drugstore. One's standing as a traveler today rises in proportion to the number of exotic entrance and exit stamps in one's passport. The "place-dropper" rules supreme. He who casually mentions Heraklion or Khorramshar is several up on the London-Paris-Rome bourgeoisie. (Now even place-dropping is getting to be a tough game to buck. The thing these days, I am told, is "airport-dropping." One no longer says he visited Teheran. He says his plane landed at Mehrabad Airport. No one in his right social mind asks "Where's that?") The prestige of having visited an exotic land was silently acknowledged by a recent advertisement of Qantas Empire Airways, Ltd. The two-page, four-color ad consisted entirely of travel stickers—including such dandies as Singapore, Jakarta, Mauritius, and Fiji—perforated for easy removal from the magazine and gummed for prompt—and *sub rosa*—application to one's suitcase.

But in the last analysis, the peripatetic is a traveler looking for something to happen to him that he can brag about when he gets home. He is like the whale that ceaselessly roams the ocean sieving tons of water through the hairy fringes of its whalebone plates in order to filter out the specks of nourishing plankton. The traveler on the move cruises in high gear, hoping that the sheer quantity of the intake of his experiences will yield at least one or two tidbits good for retelling to the folks back home.

It is a pointed commentary on the alleged pleasure we take in journeying that a disproportionate amount of this enjoyment centers on our luck or our ability in coming up with an anecdote nobody can top. The fact is that most people taking a trip wish not "to be" somewhere, but "to have been" there and to be home talking about it. "It therefore comes to pass," said the philosopher Spinoza clairvoyantly, "that everyone is fond of relating his own exploits . . . and that men are on this account a nuisance one to the other."

Certainly it cannot be disputed that much of happiness lies in anticipation and remembrance. This is especially true of travel. But just what is a memorable experience for the average pleasure traveler?

Interviewers recently asked travelers returning from Europe, "Of all the things that happened to you or that you did on this trip, what one thing stands out in your mind?" Now, you might think you could guess at least the trend of the replies: the Blue Grotto at Capri, perhaps; or the charming inn in the Cotswolds; the Wagner festival at Bayreuth; the superb dinner at L'Auberge d'Estomac Gros; or even, in a burst of honesty, that blonde in Copenhagen.

But nothing like any of these stood out in the memories of the tourists. These are the things they recalled as the outstanding incidents of their trip to Europe:

"I had my pocket picked in Rome."

"Seeing Walt Disney's circorama at the World's Fair in Brussels."

"It took so long to get our car repaired in Ireland."

"The woman in the next seat to me coming home almost died with a heart attack. I'll never forget it."

"The soul of a journey is liberty, perfect liberty, to think, feel, do just as one pleases," wrote the essayist William Hazlitt. "We go on a journey chiefly to be free of all impediments; to leave ourselves behind, much more to get rid of others."

Mr. Hazlitt, meet Mr. George O'Reilly, advertising manager for the Cunard Steamship Company, Ltd. In announcing the adoption of "Sail away to Europe on Cunard's vacation island" as the company's advertising theme for 1961, Mr. O'Reilly explained that great care was taken to avoid the use of "such a negative word as 'escape.' The 'vacation island' ad is positive. We think it suggests having a good time with a shipload of friends."

The fact is that while most travelers would probably agree in theory with Hazlitt's concept of a pleasant journey, few either can or want to carry it out in practice. Certainly not the man in the green station wagon who is accompanied on his vacation trip by his wife, three children, and six suitcases. Nor the couple who are spending only one day in Paris because months ago, when they planned their trip, they booked the midnight flight to Rome and now can't change their reservations. Nor the lady who does not feel free to enjoy herself until she has assiduously bought gifts for all the people on her list. Nor the businessman who checks in each day at the branch office of his brokerage house to see how the New York Stock Market is doing.

But, apart from all these compulsions, the single biggest obstacle to traveling Hazlitt-style today is the crowds. Despite the spread of vacation time through the year, the great bulk of holidaying is still done in July and August. Facilities of all kinds—roads, restaurants, service stations, lodgings, transportation, places of entertainment, even the countryside itself—are severely overtaxed. Those in the business of encouraging travel manfully try to expand accommodations and services while simultaneously trying to preserve the placid atmosphere that attracted visitors in the first place. But the task is virtually impossible. Last year, for example, while hotel capacity in the main tourist areas was increasing by 10 per cent, transportation capacity to those areas grew by 200 per cent. For every new jet plane that goes into service—and in 1961 there were more than two hundred of them—at least one new hotel has to be built somewhere merely to keep abreast of the housing needs of the additional travelers. "The congestion in Heaven on Judgment Day," commented a travel executive, "will probably be no greater than it is along the terrestrial strips of paradise in the peak season."

Except for the man who owns an island or a tree house, it is virtually impossible to "get rid of others." The song of the open road is drowned out by the horn-honking rush of traffic. One can drive for scores of miles along a coastline before finding an empty bit of beach to wander. I once drove for two hours across the Texas Panhandle looking for a tree in whose shade I could eat lunch. Every tree was taken. Nowhere is the overcrowding of vacation areas more obvious than in our National Parks. Each year new attendance records are set. This year nearly 100,000,000 people will descend on the Parks, almost all of them in the summer months. What should be a retreat into the stillness and beauty of the wilderness becomes a battle for survival. You rise at dawn not to see the white-tailed deer drinking at the river's edge, but to be one of the first in line to reserve a cabin for the night. It is disconcerting to try to lose yourself in the grandeur of Inspiration Point while gaggles of other tourists wait impatiently for you to move along. In Yellowstone National Park you can no longer see the bears for the people.

The loss of the pleasure of "liberty" in travel as a result of overcrowding is nobody's fault. It is a natural development of an expanding and leisured population. But the voluntary surrender of this freedom is another thing. And we are seeing that surrender occur with increasing frequency under the guise of packaged tours and group trips. It is a paradox that the main selling point of these preplanned, highly organized, and tightly scheduled caravanserais is that they give the pleasure traveler a chance to travel "free of all impediments."

Because the sheer mechanics of touring have become inordinately complex, travel agencies and transportation lines have flung themselves eagerly into the breach. "See Europe Without Running Yourself Ragged," says one airline—a fate I am sure never occurred to William Hazlitt. There are more "worry-free, all-fun" tours available than you can shake a passport at; no worries about where to go, what to see, how much to pay, who to tip, where to eat, what to say. For the elderly or the nervous, a tour may solve problems. But the average traveler is merely exchanging one set of impedimenta for another, putting a layer of insulation between himself and the experiences he is ostensibly making the trip to enjoy.

Even the unpackaged tourist sacrifices the chance for unexpected pleasures in return for the feeling that he is not a stranger in a strange land. With a thousand indigenous cafés to choose from, he heads unerringly for the local "American-style" restaurant. His eyes light up at the neon sign proclaiming "Snack Bar." And there must be some reason why so many night clubs all over the world are named for Midwestern states.

This same psychology, no doubt, accounts for the success of the American hotel chains that are building pleasure palaces overseas. How comforting to check into the Nile Hilton or the Sheraton Tel Aviv and realize that if you closed your eyes you could almost feel you were in Chicago, say, or Pittsburgh.

Chapter XI

THE WORLD OF THE "PLEASURE NEUROTIC"

And pleasure brings as surely in her train Remorse, and
Sorrow, and vindictive Pain.

—WILLIAM COWPER, *The Progress of Error*

O NE of America's most prolific and successful writers has
confessed that the quantity and scope of his literary
output is not so much the result of creative drive as it
is of the dread of pleasure. For twenty-five years, Jerome Weidman told an interviewer, he worked mornings on his best-selling novels and afternoons on his short stories. But his evenings were free, and this struck Mr. Weidman as a miscarriage
of justice. After all, he reasoned, he relished his work, and it
brought him substantial returns both of worldly goods and
worldly fame. Did he also deserve to have time in which to
enjoy himself?

In an effort to atone for the guilt he felt during the leisurely evenings, Weidman started work earlier and earlier in
the day. But even when his self-imposed schedule brought
him face to platen with his typewriter at six o'clock in the
morning, the work-free nights still nibbled at his peace of
mind. Weidman finally decided to write plays so that he

would have a legitimate excuse to labor in the evenings. The results, so far, have been two Broadway hits, with a third in the making. This may have created additional problems for Weidman's tax accountants, but the writer's own dilemma was solved: He had escaped the opportunity for pleasure.

Mr. Weidman is not alone in his quandary. Pleasure is a threat to many Americans. They go to almost any lengths to avoid it. They abhor free time because it is necessary to fill it with fun. To paraphrase the Bard, out of this flower, leisure, they pluck this nettle, duty.

Psychiatrists have a predilection for finding a skeleton in even the most proper mental closet; but there is nevertheless considerable weight of evidence to lend credence to the claim that there is a valid clinical syndrome which may be called the "pleasure neurosis," and that the fear of pleasure can be one of the symptoms of psychiatric illness.

The "pleasure neurotic" may be defined as a person who suffers from a deep psychological fear of relaxation. He is equipped, often brilliantly, for all the workaday functions of life. But he is lost when work is over. So deep is his fear of leisure that he *must* remain in harness as long as possible. The pleasure neurotic is the man who brings home enough work from the office to carry him through the awful hiatus of the evening. He is the man who can't stand Sunday. He is the man who, at the behest of his subconscious, fritters away the hours of the day so that he will have a legitimate excuse to work overtime at night. He is the slave to lists and systems and routines—devices all nicely calculated to protect him from having time on his hands. He is the man for whom pleasure is equated with the defiance of authority; this creates feelings of anxiety and guilt; the only way he can appease these feelings and that authority—which is in fact the conscience of his childhood—is by hard work. He cannot give himself permission to let down.

Faced with the threatened possibility of enjoyment, the pleasure neurotic becomes restless and irritable. Intolerant of *in*activity, he is equally unable to bear activity. To read, to watch television, to go to a movie, to hit golf balls at a driving range—these escapist recreations produce not relaxation but intense guilt feelings. Only if these pleasures can be somehow converted into *necessities*—to read for business or for self-improvement; to watch a program or a picture so that one can discuss it intelligently at the office next day; to hit golf balls to improve one's waistline—only then can they be indulged in without the penalty of penitence.

The pleasure neurotic, as a result, takes part in enjoyable activities only furtively or defiantly. Either avenue leads inevitably to a deeper guilt. On occasion the pleasure neurotic secretly savors the delicious possibility of not only *not* enjoying himself, but of simultaneously being able to delude himself about his true motives and thereby to feel martyred for having to "give up" the pleasures he does not want in the first place.

Deliberately, the pleasure neurotic sets himself impossible schedules calling for enormous stints of concentrated endeavors. One of the most incredibly such work-oriented persons was the late Dr. Douglas Southall Freeman. He was the shirt-sleeve editor of a distinguished daily newspaper. He was the commentator for a twice-daily radio news program. He was a famous biographer; his four-volume study of General Robert E. Lee had won a Pulitzer Prize. For many years he combined with all these intensely demanding tasks the teaching of a one-day-a-week course in editorial journalism—an assignment that required him to commute from his home in Richmond, Virginia, to his New York City classroom in time to begin lecturing at eight o'clock in the morning.

To accomplish all this, Douglas Freeman lived by a schedule that ordinary men would find fantastic, if not downright impossible. He arose every day at 3:15 in the morning. By 4:40 he was in his newspaper office studying the news developments in preparation for the task of writing several thousand words of editorials—a job that on comparable papers would be a full day's work for several men. Freeman's editorial deadline was 7:58, for at eight his first radio program began. From 8:17 to noon he worked on the paper's affairs, and then strolled to a microphone for his second news broadcast. Having finished the first eight hours of his standard seventeen-hour working day, Freeman went home for lunch and an extremely brief nap. By 1 P.M. he was ready to work on his current book. At 6 P.M. Freeman dined with his wife and three children. This was the only time during the day that he saw any of them. By 8 P.M. Freeman was in bed in his own room. When he was teaching or lecturing, Freeman stepped up this pace sufficiently to enable him to turn out in advance his editorials and his daily stint on his book. Freeman not only planned his schedule with precision and carried it out with iron discipline; he also kept a notebook listing a minute-by-minute account of the time devoted to his various activities. He gave up smoking because he calculated that the time spent in purchasing cigarettes, lighting them, and puffing them used up eight hours a week unproductively.

This kind of intensive flight from leisure differs chiefly in degree, rather than in kind, from the evasive action taken by the millions of Americans who are plagued with vague fears and uneasy feelings at the prospect of pleasure. Two Purdue sociologists have even indicted the entire American middle class as the perpetrators of an emotional crime they have labeled the Deferred Gratification Pattern. "Middle class persons," say Louis Schneider and Sverre Lysgaard, "feel they should save, postpone or renounce a variety of gratifications. They delay economic independence through an elaborate process of education; they tend to defer sexual gratification through intercourse; and they show a marked tendency to save money."

From earliest childhood, with its emphasis on "growing up" and "taking on responsibilities," we are taught to eschew the pleasure principle. We seek approval from teachers and parents, and the straightest path to approval is to be industrious and obedient. As the twig is bent, so grows the tree. As adults, we transfer these attitudes to our employers. "Americans seem to work on the principle of postponement," says Dr. Alexander Wolf. "They drive themselves by saying, 'Someday I will be able to have pleasures, but now I must work.' It is never themselves they must satisfy, but always others. Their own enjoyment is postponed."

In his book, *The Stress of Life*, Dr. Hans Selye points out in pity how "so many people work hard and intelligently for some immediate objective which promises leisure to enjoy life tomorrow, and tomorrow never becomes today. There is always another objective which promises even more leisure in exchange for just a little more work. Hence, very few people . . . attain the ability really to enjoy themselves . . . But it hurts to be conscious of this defect, so adults dope themselves with more work to divert attention from their loss."

This kind of "impulse renunciation" can be seen in the driving and driven executive who refused to take time off until he became so tense that his doctor had to hospitalize him to force him to rest; or in the woman who wanted more than anything in the world to learn to play the violin—and who promised herself every day that she would really do so if she ever got sick and, thus, had the time free for such frivolity. Impulse renunciation reaches its peak in those who are unable to permit themselves the pleasure of a vacation. Psychiatrist Dr. Alexander Reid Martin, chairman of the Committee on Leisure-Time Activities of the American Psychiatric Association, tells of a patient whose duodenal ulcer pains became violently aggravated when he was not working. The man desperately tried to take a vacation. But as soon as he began to make the routine preparations—buying plane tickets, making hotel reservations—he would be stricken with severe pains. Several times he attempted to ignore the pain and go ahead with his plans, but it intensified until he was compelled to undergo bed rest and sedation. A couple of days later, when it was too late to do anything about rescheduling the vacation, the ulcer pains went away.

"One way a pleasure neurotic has of dealing with this situation," says Dr. Martin, "is to take a rest, go off on a holiday, play games, have recreation—but always proceed to be rather miserable and unhappy, and see to it that there is no enjoyment. The principle here is that you don't have to pay in guilt for what you don't enjoy. Of course, the whole maneuver is a piece of gross deception."

Most pleasure neurotics, however, experience nothing much stronger than the Saturday morning stirrings of a conscience pricked by the prospect of forty-eight duty-free hours. These, however, are bad enough. The weekend, psychiatrists report, "is the time when Americans fall victim to accidents of all sorts, and when hostilities between married couples are seen to break out into the open"—a conclusion presumably adjusted to compensate for the extra automobile mileage and martini consumption that mark the nation's days of rest. The phrase "weekend neurosis" is now a commonplace of psychiatric jargon.

The chief dilemma of the weekend pleasure neurotic is, of course, to find that strait and narrow path that will at once assuage his fears of relaxation yet at the same time enable him to pay lip service to the convention of *dolce far niente*. Advertisers, normally notoriously unconcerned with matters of conscience, intuitively recognize this critical situation and heroically hurl themselves into the breach.

Thus a manufacturer of waxes which require no rubbing or buffing—or, anyway, practically none—urges you to "set a morning aside, some weekend soon"—and give your car a rubdown. The headline—"Call It Escape, If You Like"—is reassuring. It puts the socially acceptable face on the psychologically needful but traditionally anti-social act. Another advertiser, no doubt on the advice of more daring motivation experts, does not beat about the bush even that much. He shows us a typical American male, dressed in sports shirt, slacks, and a broad anticipatory grin, and laden with garden hose, hedge trimmers, trowel, seed packets, and lawnmower, obviously heading to cultivate his garden. As any homeowner knows, this man is embarking on several hours of back-breaking, knee-grinding, muscle-wrenching labor. (And as any sociologist knows, as we have seen from their studies of gardens, our hero is doing this more for the neighbors than for his own enjoyment.) But the ad copy, wise to the ways of the pleasure neurotic, blithely says: "There's a long wonderful weekend coming up!"

Pleasure neurosis is not a new phenomenon, nor an exclusive product of our leisured times. More than forty years ago the psychoanalyst Sandor Ferenczi was treating patients who had nervous ailments that attacked them only on specific days of the week, and which recurred regularly on those days.

"Most of the patients experienced these periodical returns of the disturbances on Sundays," wrote Ferenczi. "They were mostly headaches or stomach disturbances that were wont to appear on this day without any particular cause, and often utterly spoiled the person's one free day of the week."

Ferenczi labeled this phenomenon "Sunday neurosis." He attributed it to his patients' inability to "vent their holiday wantonness freely," either because they were conscience-stricken about being at leisure, or because they felt it necessary to closely guard impulses which would otherwise run

riot. The result, said Ferenczi, was "untimely depression and
. . . little hysterical symptoms" such as the Sunday aches
and pains.

But the social and economic progress that has taken place
since Ferenczi has made it possible for today's pleasure
neurotics to be emotionally and physically ill at ease for two
days instead of one. And on the horizon looms the prospect
of three days each week of "untimely depression" and "little
hysterical symptoms."

This gloomy prognosis is not without basis in fact. For
example, a few years ago the well-meaning executives of a
small aircraft-manufacturing plant in Southern California
decided to give each employee a three-day weekend once
every four weeks. The theory of this laboratory experiment
in concentrated pleasure was that a man and his family would
have a chance to relax thoroughly; perhaps to get away to the
beaches or the mountains which, in Southern California, are
at most only a few hours' drive distant; perhaps to embark on
a project such as a camping or hiking trip which might be
overly ambitious for a two-day weekend. In order to maintain
plant production under this setup, the schedule also had to
call for each employee to put in one extra day each month
to earn the long weekend.

Plant executives were concerned about employee reaction
to the idea of that one six-day week. But, to their amaze-
ment, the bulk of the complaints was directed against the
four-day week.

The responsibility to have pleasure weighed heavily. Most
employees either feared it or did not know how to use it: "I
get up, take a shower, by that time it's noon, so I have lunch,
maybe work around the yard, work on the house, work on the
car—that's about all," one man said.

"That long weekend is for the birds," another reported.
"It's a terrible thing, just a terrible thing. A man shouldn't

have all that time. A three-day weekend is just too much. By
the time Monday night came I was just dying to get back to
work."

"Too much time off," a third employee said, "and you
start gettin' lazy."

Employees' wives didn't like the three-day weekend either.
"I have too much work to do around the house," one said.
"If my husband's home all that time, he gets in the way."

After several months during which the grousing increased
rather than tapered off, a plant-wide ballot was held. Employees voted overwhelmingly against the "long weekend"
plan. To satisfy its curiosity, the company called in sociologists
and asked them to see if they could find out why the scheme
had failed.

The experts ultimately reported that so-called "controlled"
persons liked the long weekend. They were the ones who
thought ahead, who bought camping equipment, planned
trips, made reservations. The "uncontrolled" persons—in the
vast majority—would wake up on Saturday morning, suddenly
realize the three-day weekend was upon them, and be panicked
at the expanse of free time they faced.

It is not relaxation or enjoyment per se that the pleasure
neurotic seeks to put, like Satan, behind him. By his own
testimony such pitiful devices as spending an entire Saturday
shopping for next week's food supplies are enthusiastically
labeled "fun." "My wife and I," said a man recently interviewed for a food-page feature in the *New York Times*,
"make Saturday our regular shopping junket." (Note the art-
ful subconscious use of the word "junket," with its connotations of carousing.) "We come here to the supermarket for
our staples. Next we'll go to the sidewalk markets for fruit
and vegetables. Then we'll go down to get some wonderful
Italian sausage. Oh, we make a day of it."

Behind this façade of puerile jollity lies the pleasure neurotic's real *bête noire*—his fear, as Dr. Martin explains, "of the impulses and feelings that would emerge if he relaxed his compulsion to busy-ness." Presumably these impulses are basically hostile or even dangerous to the individual or those around him. One worried weekender put it this way: "You have time off, you start to think up things to do; pretty soon it gets easy to think up things you *shouldn't* do."

But activity removes the need for thinking, deadens anxiety, and throws a sop to the emotions. Just as the new bulk cellulose diets promised for the nation's overweight millions will fill the stomach without nourishing the body, so hustle and bustle fill the pleasure neurotic's free time without providing fun or relaxation.

Psychoanalysts have only recently begun to explore the paradoxical relationship between constant busyness and the incapacity for enjoyment. But it was known to philosophers as long ago as the Middle Ages when they formulated the concept of the sin of Acedia—sloth, laziness, spiritual apathy. From it, writes Aldous Huxley, "comes dread to begin to work any good deeds . . . the sense of universal futility, the feelings of boredom and despair." In short, the inability to enjoy leisure.

Acedia, however, according to such philosophers of leisure and pleasure as Joseph Pieper, is a more subtle vice than mere physical or mental indolence. It leads, on the contrary, to restlessness and to leisurelessness. "Metaphysically," says Pieper, "the notion of acedia means that a man does not give the consent of his will to his own being; that behind or beneath the activity of his existence, he is still not at one with himself . . . In a word, he does not want to be as God wants him to be, and that ultimately means that he does not wish to be what he fundamentally is . . . He is thus a prey to sadness." And, inevitably, also to that "deep-seated lack of calm which makes leisure impossible."

What Pieper pointed out theoretically the analysts have tried to explain symptomatically. The hyperactivity that characterizes the pleasure neurotic is, they say, an inner defense against the constant threat of boredom and the incapacity to enjoy pleasure.

For the common property of boredom is not resignation, but expectation; boredom thrives when something does *not* occur, when there is no stimulus to provoke a reaction. Thus analyst Otto Fenichel, discussing the pleasure neurotics, observed that "so long as they are at work, these people succeed in diverting themselves from their state of pent-up drives. When the diversion is not possible, the tension makes itself felt in boredom."

Liquor and tobacco are among the standard indulgences used to discharge some of this tension. "But," Alexander Martin points out, "we have gone a long way from the good old days of the pipe and the bowl and the fiddlers three. Now, too many are compelled to drink and smoke to relieve their fear of even brief moments of free time."

Compulsive drinking and smoking are both indicative and symptomatic of that fear. The club car on trains and bar service on planes save large numbers of travelers from the fate of having to pass substantial amounts of time with only their inner resources to carry them through. Perhaps railroad magnates might investigate the theory that part of the decline in long-haul passenger traffic is attributable to the difficulty many people have merely in passing day after day in the solitude of their compartments.

The increased amounts of drinking and smoking people do on vacation, or in resort areas, is not necessarily so much a letting down the bars as it is the raising of a barrier. The social rituals that go with the drink and the smokes are magic gestures designed to draw a pentagram of safety around the pleasure neurotic, to keep at bay for a few extra moments the reality of leisure time. The compulsive nature of a good deal of social drinking has been documented. The compulsive nature of smoking has been largely taken for granted. But few persons, outside of cigar smokers and people in television commercials—have ever been heard to say they *enjoy* the taste of tobacco. With what is being done to cigarettes today in the form of ever-milder, ever-more-blended mixtures, plus increased filtration that sometimes makes it a struggle just to get the smoke past the Carcinogenic Curtain, it is well-nigh impossible to tell whether a cigarette *has* any taste at all. They are smoked almost exclusively out of habit, out of the need to give lips and hands something to do. If proof were needed, it is available in the existence of a new company which is going to manufacture *half* a cigarette. An artfully hinged package will hold forty half-cigarettes—especially made for folks who take only a symptomatic puff or two before throwing the fag away.

Medical science is also coming to the rescue of the pleasure neurotic. More than fifty million prescriptions are written annually for tranquilizing pills. Heaven knows how many million more are written for sleeping pills, or how many million patent-medicine substitutes are sold over the drugstore counters. The escape from pleasure now comes in capsules.

In the future, we may look back upon the capsules as relics of a saner age. For not far distant is the possibility that we can be delivered from the dilemma altogether—that we can spend our leisure plugged in to a pleasure machine, having sixty-cycle ecstasies delivered via silver-wire electrodes implanted in the pleasure center of our brain.

Science has long known that specific areas in the cortex of the brain control specific motor and sensory systems—

sight, speech, touch, hearing, and so forth. Science has long assumed that to expect similar focal points for the "higher feelings"—notably pain, pleasure, fear, and love—was at best naïve and at worst superstitious.

But experimenters have proven that the relatively un-explored midbrain does house specific centers for such re-actions as sleep; the emergency "fight or flight" reaction; and such emotional behavior as pain or pleasure responses. In a series of tests at McGill University physiologists proved be-yond doubt the existence of pleasure centers in the brain. Electrodes were implanted in the brains of rats. When plugged into a circuit, the animal could be given—or, by pressing a treadle with its paw could give itself—electrical stimulation of various areas in the midbrain region. The "do-it-yourself" technique enabled the experimenters to measure an animal's desire for such stimulation by the frequency with which it voluntarily pressed the treadle.

"When the electrodes were implanted in the classical sensory and motor systems," wrote scientist James Olds, "re-sponse rates stayed at the chance level of 10 to 25 an hour. In most parts of the mid-line (mid-brain) system, the re-sponse rates rose to levels of from 200 to 5000 an hour, definitely indicative of a rewarding effect of the electric stimulus. But in some of the lower parts . . . there was an opposite effect: the animal would press the lever once and never go back. This indicated a punishing effect in those areas. They appeared to be the same areas where . . . others had found responses of rage and escape. The animals seemed to experience the strongest reward, or pleasure, from stimu-lation of regions found to be centers for control of digestive, sexual, excretory and similar processes."

If the electrode was in or near the bull's-eye of the pleasure center, the rat much preferred to stand there and keep shock-ing itself than it did to eat. Some rats, even after being kept for hours without food, hurried not to saucers of bran mash but to the treadle of the electric stimulator. One animal sent the current coursing through its pleasure center more than two thousand times an hour for twenty-four consecutive hours.

What did the scientists conclude? First, that "brain stimulation in these regions must excite some of the nerve cells that would be excited by satisfaction of the basic drives—hunger, sex, thirst, and so forth." Second, that "emotional mechanisms can indeed be localized in the brain; that certain portions of the brain are sensitive to each of the basic drives." Third—and most significant—that "enough of the brain-stimulating work has been repeated on monkeys to indicate that our general conclusions can very likely be generalized eventually to human beings. . . ."

With these sober statements from conservative scientists already on the record, it is not too hard to believe in the apocalyptic science-fiction vision of humanity living out its years in self-contained cocoons, yielding completely to the sensations produced by the electrical tickling of its pleasure centers.

Chapter XII

THE SEARCH FOR PLEASURE

"You say: 'They wouldn't know how best to waste their days!' Believe me, each one of them has his own occupation, and even one on which he has wasted his whole life, and not merely a day. Certainly you cannot blame each one of them for the fact that he was unable to carve a paradise out of his life, and that, in consequence, he is suffering. Well, it pleases me to look at these sufferers here, and to watch them laughing."

"Don't they laugh out of mere politeness?"

"They laugh by force of habit which . . . compels them to play their part in the 'game of paradise.' They do not believe in paradise, and they are playing this game reluctantly, but still they are playing it, and this amuses them. The habit is too deeply rooted. Here you will find some people who are taking it seriously—and, of course, this is all the better for them: they feel as if they were in a real paradise. If you love them all (and you must love them) you must rejoice over the fact that they are given a chance to rest and forget themselves, even though in a mirage."

—FEODOR DOSTOEVSKI, *Diary of a Writer*

AMERICA is the only country where pleasure is a problem, and where the problem is so solemnly debated. Most of the world is too busy, poor, hungry, sick, weary, or oppressed even to think of pleasure. The minority for whom a modicum of enjoyment out of life is possible do not worry pleasure as a dog worries a bone; they do what comes naturally. Only in America is pleasure a matter for scrutiny and breast-beating. Scholars of Olympian repute spend days in earnest panel discussions about "meaningful values for the leisure revolution." Sociologists research pleasure; psychiatrists analyze it; foundations publish reports about it; the President of the United States, when he is not busy with the Cold War or civil rights, expresses official concern regarding it; and at least four major national organizations exist to cope with it.

The Indian writer Santha Rama Rau once was inveigled into taking part in a conference on the uses of leisure. She listened for many hours to speakers most of whom viewed with alarm the prospect of a nation with five billion leisure hours to fill every week. Her own comment provided perspective. "Surely nowhere else in the world," she said, "do people fuss so much about what to do in their spare time . . . What is wrong with lying on the beach?"

Yet there are many reasons why Americans dissect pleasure. For one thing, we are fascinated by social self-analysis. For another, we are growing to be a stuffy people who look upon leisure and pleasure not as delights to be accepted but as responsibilities to be discharged. Management fusses because proposals for a shorter working week are almost invariably coupled with proposals for a higher rate of pay. Labor unions fuss because workers are more interested in money, and what it will buy, than they are in more time off. Some people wonder whether the ratio of work to pleasure should not be a matter of national policy rather than personal preference in these critical times. If, they say, during the next ten years a total of two hours is subtracted from the average work-week, our Gross National Product will suffer by fifty billion dollars. Others point out with equal logic that what counts is not the *amount* of the GNP, but the kinds of goods and services it includes, and the uses to which they are put. Perhaps all of this—including our individual qualms and personal misgivings about fun—stems from the root fact that we are *nouveau riche* when it comes to leisure. Therefore we vacillate between graceless uses and boorish displays of pleasure at one extreme, and self-conscious concern about it at the other.

Some of us suffer from well-ordered boredom; William Faulkner once described this thorn in the side of leisure. "One of the saddest things," he said, "is that the only thing a man can do for eight hours a day is work. You can't eat eight hours a day nor drink eight hours a day nor make love eight hours a day—all you can do for eight hours is work. Which is why man makes himself and everybody else so miserable and unhappy."

Others suffer from impatience; they demand *immediate* satisfaction from a pleasurable activity. Sophocles observed that one must wait until the evening to see how splendid the day was. Yet many people cannot wait for a long-term reward. Most of us, however, suffer from a surfeit of potential pleasures. The sociologist Gunnar Myrdal in his study of the American Negro pointed out that the Negro had so little time free from labor, and was cut off by segregation from so many forms of recreation available to white people, that he perforce learned to enjoy whatever simple pleasures were available to him. Americans today—to an increasing degree regardless of color—have so many divertisements at hand that we can afford to be eternally disenchanted. We need not enjoy *this* because there is always *that*; we need not take pleasure in *that*, because there is always something else.

The Utopian assumptions about pleasure have crumbled beneath the dead weight of the facts. Thomas More, predicting a society with a six-hour working day, took it for granted that all men would find their joys in tending gardens, in conversation, in leisurely travel, in the cultivation of the mind.

Other romantics envisioned the liberated working class strolling through the fields at eventide discussing literature and philosophy.

Do not smile. These visionaries were not so far wrong in attributing to man the desire for such pleasures. Where the Utopians erred was in expecting that men would actually do what they said they wanted to do. When interviewers ask people today what they want to do for pleasure that they are *not* doing, the answers are much along Utopian lines: they want to read good books, to travel, study, quietly commune with loved ones. But what do these people actually do? They spend nearly four billion hours a week watching television and listening to the radio. And what would they do if they had an *extra* two hours every day all to themselves? Sociologist Alfred C. Clarke asked this question a few years ago of several thousand men whom he classified into "prestige levels" on the basis of their jobs. At the lower end of the scale—unskilled and semi-skilled workers—more than half would use this extra time to "loaf, sleep or work around the house." Even among small-business proprietors and white-collar workers these were the pleasure choices of 40 per cent. Only at the top level of executives and professional men was "reading and study" the first choice. And even among *them*, 25 per cent said they'd use two additional hours to loaf and sleep.

Statistics like these both horrify and delight tight groups of well-meaning specialists whom, for lack of a more generic term, I shall call pleasure-crats. They are people poised to invade and conquer our most private citadel—our time. Pleasure-crats are people who think that Americans need to be taught how to enjoy themselves, and who think that *they* are the ones best qualified to do the teaching. It would be heartening to know that so many people feel competent to lead us into the land of leisure milk and honey were it not for a few cautionary facts. One is that, like Moses, none of them really know in which direction it lies. Another is that almost all of them have private, institutional axes to grind. A third is that many (consciously or not) seek the power that would inevitably accrue to any group which dominated the national philosophy of pleasure.

Not long ago Mr. Willard C. Sutherland of the National Recreation Association made this revealing statement: "Since the average citizen is unable to invent new uses for his leisure, a professional elite shares a heavy responsibility for discovering criteria for ways of employing leisure and creating enthusiasms." There have been mild suggestions that Americans could use "avocational counselors." There have been clarion calls for government to assume "the responsibility of educating our people to use their free time constructively . . . lest tremendous new energies be turned against us." It has been seriously proposed that the President's Cabinet include a Secretary of Leisure. Other would-be pleasure-crats have not been quite so coy. They have given as their opinion (though not in so many words) that the average person is a clod who does not know what to do with a day off and must be told or trained by his betters. Thus a New England industrialist once declared: "We must think in terms of taking the whole person and budgeting the whole time; in other words, forecasting the time by saying what the hours will be, you forecast for them by helping them prepare for their leisure time." A recreation leader wrote that group pleasures were "of higher value" than those enjoyed alone—a philosophy reminiscent of the attitude of totalitarian states, where people are not encouraged to be alone, and where pleasure consists of mass activities.

There is no lack of eager volunteers to staff the cadres of

this "professional elite." Indeed, the jostling for position is already underway.

Among the market-place-minded, for example, from theoretical economists to shirt-sleeve advertising men, the solution to all problems of pleasure is, as we have seen, consumerism unlimited. Their motto is: *When in doubt—buy!* Yet, observes psychologist Erich Fromm, if a man "consumes commodities in an alienated way, how can he make use of his leisure time in an active and meaningful way . . . His leisure-time consumption is determined by industry . . . he is made to buy fun as he buys dresses and shoes . . . Something happens within myself when I am reading, looking at scenery . . . I am not the same after the experience as I was before. In the alienated form of pleasure nothing happens within me; I have consumed this or that; nothing is changed within myself. . . ."

At the other extreme some educators, pointing out that the Greek word for leisure is *skole*, hold that the broadening of personal horizons through learning is the only valid use of free time, and the only lasting pleasure. Like motherhood, education in the arts and the humanities cannot be denigrated. On the other hand, it can be overdone. It was all very well for the Greek freeman, who had little of the world's work to do except order his slaves about, to spend his leisure in intellectual explorations. But most of us today cannot afford to do this even if we want to.

No one will deny that a liberal arts education—as opposed to one that trains specifically for work—is an advantage in the search for pleasure. That our young people should be educated in recreation and prepared to live an esthetically rewarding life is a nice theory. But all too often, these days, what passes for the liberal arts is a conglomeration of "life adjustment" courses that may range from music appreciation to driver training, from clay manipulation to skiing. At a time when many high school seniors cannot read, write, nor spell properly, and when parents are deeply concerned about getting their youngsters into good colleges, these kinds of "frill courses" give a bad name to the entire concept of education for pleasure.

Psychiatrists lay a special claim to the right to be teachers of pleasure. It is, they say, merely an extension of their present function of treating mental patients with recreational therapy. In working with the mentally disturbed, the psychiatrist's aim is to redirect troublesome emotions into socially approved outlets. Dr. William A. Menninger described, for example, how a man who hated his father was encouraged to bash away at a punching bag that had the father's picture painted on it. Another man had a long list of people *he* hated, so the psychiatrists had him go each day to a golf driving range and tee off on balls that were given the names of the persons he disliked. A compulsive neurotic who made life unbearable for himself and his family by his insistence on precision and orderliness was encouraged to become a stamp collector—an acceptable compulsion.

Now, all this is very well until psychiatrists start saying, as some of them do, that the problem of pleasure is really a public health issue; and that their experience with recreational therapy for mental patients fits them to guide recreation in the community at large. "The important difference between recreation inside and outside the hospital," says a booklet published by the Group for the Advancement of Psychiatry, "results from the fact that for hospital patients leisure is enforced while for healthy individuals it is elective." But if the pleasure-crats of psychiatry have their way, this "important difference" may ultimately be blurred into extinction, and leisure-time activities be just as enforced for one group as for the other.

For example, Dr. Menninger has flatly stated that "the

best kind of recreation must be learned. Personality characteristics and psychological needs are the basis for the appeal
of certain types of play. And the maximum satisfaction comes
from instruction." Dr. George S. Stevenson, an authority on
mental health, said that persons who tend to be tense, busy,
or bored may need to take recreation as a duty. "Get someone
to schedule your recreation as you would schedule a business
appointment," he wrote, "and have that someone push or
pull you out to the golf course, concert or whatever. Once
you've done this a few times the habit will become automatic." One wonders how this ingenuous prescription for enforced pleasure will mitigate either tension or monotony.

But the most highly organized of the pleasure-crats today
are the professional recreationists. Compared to the mer-
chandiser, who sees pleasure as a potential bonanza; to the
educator, who sees it as an opportunity to raise cultural
standards; and to the psychiatrist, who sees it as therapy—
compared to all these, the recreationist is a man with a simple
but wholesome device on his banner: his answer to the search
for pleasure is for everybody to get out there and *play!*

Nothing is such a challenge to a recreationist as the sight
of a body at rest. The handbooks of the field list literally
hundreds of activities to fill free time. These range from
weight-lifting to letter-writing, hopscotch to night-clubbing,
sand sculpture to kazoo playing. The recreationist can call a
square dance at the drop of a do-si-do. He knows the difference
between "continuous" and "non-continuous" tag. He knows
special songs to pep up meetings. A real livener-upper, for
instance, is *Three Blind Mice* sung in action ("Three"—
raise arms high, hold up three fingers on each hand; "*blind*"
—clap hands over eyes; "mice"—pull up pants leg or dress,
stand on tiptoe, stare down in imaginary horror.) And those
temporarily on the sidelines during a game can't just stand

and watch—they must clap, sing, cheer, keep score. In motion there is merriment.

There is no harm in this approach to pleasure so long as it is kept within bounds, and applied where it can be useful. There is a real need for trained recreation leaders in camps, parks, playgrounds, hospitals, youth groups, schools, the armed forces. The harm can be done if this everybody-out-for-volleyball attitude insinuates itself into the pleasure of individuals rather than groups.

The recreationist today is all too eager to shoulder the responsibility of teaching Americans how to play. To begin with, he is seeking to dignify his work as a profession. More than sixty-five colleges give full four-year courses leading to Bachelor's, Master's, and even Doctor of Philosophy degrees in recreation. The catch is that all save a handful of these courses are in departments of physical education, and are oriented almost entirely toward sports and games. Students take tests on such subjects as badminton rules: "When using the Eastern forehand grip, the top plate of the handle comes in the middle of the V made by thumb and forefinger—True or False?" "In announcing a badminton score, whose score is given first?" Ph.D. theses are written on such topics as "The Validity of the Miller Forehand-Backhand Test for Beginning Tennis Players," and "A Comparison of the Correlations with the First Centroid Factor and with the Composite Criterion in the Wall Bounce Test." This pseudo-scholarly attitude is carried over into "research studies." Recreationists made one elaborate survey that "proved," for example, that as men get older they tend to give up such pleasures as calisthenics, weight-lifting, and casual dating. They can also tell you to within a few decimal points what percentage of men and women between eighteen and thirty-five spend their free time hiking, collecting dolls, or playing in a fife and drum corps.

To a considerable extent the professional recreationist is a Frank Merriwell type. He is high-spirited. He observes the proprieties—such as whose score to call first in a badminton game. He feels that the game is the thing; a civic leader in Kenya recently wrote to an American recreation official outlining his plans to impress the new government, which for the first time would include African politicians, with the importance of recreation: "Sometimes," he said, "one feels our African population gets depressed at seeing ahead of them a long dreary climb towards the distant goal of economic and political parity. It is then that we will try to show them the meaning of the old proverb, 'All work and no play makes Jack a dull boy.'" It will be interesting to see what reaction this provokes from the Mau Mau tribesmen.

Finally, although the recreationist realizes there are other things in life besides recreation, he knows what is *important*. For example, one leader in the field recently suggested a "well-balanced" game program to take people's minds off the H-bomb; another set up a table of organization for an emergency recreation program in the event of a nuclear war.

Recreationists are adept at guiding hobbyists and running games; but whether they are yet equipped to lead the American search for pleasure is something else again. Their answer to the problem might well be to start a potato race.

The danger in the pleasure-crat is that, although he pays lip service to the ideal of freedom of choice, the logical end result of his endeavors can well be the loss of freedom of pleasure. Play is first and foremost a voluntary activity. When it becomes a ritual, or a duty, or a bore, it loses the name of play. The liberty of the individual is, after all, not only economic or political or religious; it is, as George Orwell put it, also "the liberty to do what you like in your spare time, to choose your own amusements instead of having them chosen for you from above." Without making invidious comparisons, it is interesting that in Soviet Russia the state has become a sort of super-pleasure-crat. Leisure time is controlled almost as firmly as other facets of life. It is filled either with culturally rewarding activities or with enforced rest to give the citizen "strength for new labors" (the Puritan Communists!).

Make no mistake: for all his emphasis on fun, the pleasure-crat is most often at heart a disciple of "useful" pleasure. Perhaps he would have it build the body or relax the mind; perhaps he would have it teach sportsmanship, which he naïvely believes can be carried over from the athletic field to other areas of life (shutting his eyes to the fact that the best sport in the softball game can be the biggest heel at the office). The pleasure-crat is determined to improve us, to give us "purposeful experiences." "You cannot mean you are happy lying on the beach," he says despite our protests— and he puts forth a score of things we *should* be doing.

But the greatest threat posed by the pleasure-crat is that he makes us feel that the enjoyment of pleasure is a natural attribute of man; that it is some mysterious faculty we are endowed with at birth; and that it is a personal failure if we do not exercise it.

To teach man to have pleasure presupposes that man is meant to have pleasure.

And yet I am not at all sure that man is a creature designed to enjoy himself.

We function best under stress. Our bodies contain mechanisms magnificently designed to implement our fundamental "fight-or-flight" reaction. In danger, under pressure, the heart beats faster, the sensory organs grow more alert, energy-giving sugar is automatically released into the faster-flowing bloodstream, the metabolic rate rises, muscle fatigue is diminished. Our body almost instantaneously adapts, ready to run or to do battle. Most of these changes are triggered by the flow of adrenalin. It is interesting to speculate why man is equipped with adrenal glands, and not with any gland in his body that produces a soothing secretion, one that would encourage lassitude and relaxation.

But there is no "happiness" gland. For tranquillity we have to go to the drugstore.

Difficulties we have always been able to cope with. It is prosperity that gives us problems. The easy life troubles the conscience. Being free to have fun makes us nervous. There is a sneaking suspicion, somewhere in the deeps of the mind, that happiness is a myth and the goal of pleasure unattainable.

Yet habit hopefully compels us to play our parts—sometimes crass, sometimes stupid, often pitiable, occasionally gay —in "the game of paradise," whether or not we believe it can ever be won; whether or not we really dare to presume that pleasure is a privilege and a right of man.